Encountering the Self

Encountering the Self
Transformation & Destiny
in the Ninth Year

Hermann Koepke

Translated by Jesse Darrell

Anthroposophic Press

This book is a translation of the second edition of *Das neunte Lebensjahr*. The German original was published in 1985 by the Philosophisch-Anthroposophischer Verlag at the Goetheanum in Dornach, Switzerland. The Anthroposophic Press would like to thank the German publisher and the author for kindly granting permission to translate the German text into English.

Published by
SteinerBooks / Anthroposophic Press
www.steinerbooks.org

© 1989 Anthroposophic Press

Koepke, Hermann.
(Nuente Lebensjahr English)
Encountering the Self: transformation & destiny in the ninth year.
Hermann Koepke: translated by Jesse Darrell.
Hudson, N.Y.: Anthroposophic Press, 1989.
Translation of: Das nuente Lebensjahr.
Includes bibliographical references.
ISBN 978-0-88010-279-7
1. Waldorf method of education. 2. Child development.
3. Education—Philosophy. I. Title.
LB1029.W34K6413 1989
371.3—dc20   89-39079
                                                                    CIP

10 9

Printed in the United States of America

Contents

Part Three: Appendices

Preface to the English Edition

Since *Encountering the Self* by Hermann Koepke first appeared in German in 1983, numerous teachers in the English-speaking world realized with a certain longing that it probably could provide new insights for their work with children between the ages of nine and ten. In the Waldorf Schools the curriculum developed by Rudolf Steiner for each grade relates intimately to the age of the children. The children would be nine years old in the third grade. Since formal schooling in most non-European schools—state-supported and independent—generally begins when the child is six or even five years old, a discrepancy arises in regard to chronological age, grade level, and curriculum. Not only does *Encountering the Self* explore this important time in the child's development in general, but it also contains specific indications that will assist teachers and parents in recognizing the changes occurring during this developmental phase regardless of the child's grade level in school. Indeed, teachers will be helped in arranging their studies and activities with the children so that this discrepancy between age, grade level, and curriculum can be minimized.

We are indebted to Jesse Darrell, a Waldorf School teacher of many years in England, for a translation of this work that remains true to the German in meaning but reads as if the original language were English. Such a lucid and stylistically readable translation will serve to make *Encountering the Self* accessible to parents and educators throughout the English-speaking world.

September 1988   Virginia Sease

Acknowledgments

I would like to thank all those who have drawn the attention of so many parents to this little book that a new edition has become necessary in a very short time. Thereby they have given a helping hand to a great number of children in this critical age of life. In this second edition the chapter "Dear Parents" has been revised and enlarged. Thanks to the cooperation of Dr. Walter Holtzapfel the section "A Word from the School Doctor" could now be included. He gives important and stimulating indications out of his very long experience, thus meeting the wishes of many parents.

Easter 1985   Hermann Koepke

Foreword

In the life of every one of us there is an important turning point between the ages of nine and ten: more consciously experienced in one, and less so in another. Something intervenes at that time that works as a determining factor in the further destiny of the human being. Although Rudolf Steiner often drew attention to this event in his fundamental writings on Waldorf education, not much has been published that bears particularly upon this event.

Hermann Koepke has discovered that a reversal in the threefold human being takes place in this phase of childhood, a reversal through which the ego takes further hold of the bodily organization.

This book grew out of the author's experience of fifteen years teaching in a Rudolf Steiner School and many seminar courses in Waldorf education, so that one would gladly put it into the hands of as many parents as possible. It begins with conversations between parents and teacher. By way of actual examples, the author shows how one can help the child through the particular situation at about the ninth year, so that at this critical turning point in life the child can take in the ego in such a way that a foundation is laid for the future development toward freedom.

Jörgen Smit

Introduction

I had just hung the big watercolor paintings of the children in my first grade on the wall when Gerda Langen, an older colleague, came into the classroom. She stood there looking at the pictures with evident delight. Then she turned to me and said, "You don't need to worry when your children lose these rich powers of fantasy later on. They'll come back again, though in quite a different form." This statement and others that followed are still quite vivid in my memory, even if not word for word, and they were the first promptings that led to this little book.

As an experienced teacher, Gerda was well aware of how the powers of earlier childhood ultimately disappear. While observing students in a state school during her training as a teacher, she had noticed the difference between the sunny, happy faces of the younger children as they came to school, and the pale, dulled, almost unhealthy looks of the older ones. As it dawned on her that these children had lost their best forces after they had begun school, she had to ask herself whether in fact she could go on and become a teacher herself. "While weighed down by this problem," she explained, "I went to a lecture of Rudolf Steiner's and something extraordinary happened. It was as if he turned away from the theme he was pursuing in order to say something about the question that was occupying me. He spoke of a stream that meanders away and vanishes into the ground, only to reappear elsewhere and continue its course. He compared this phenomenon in nature with certain soul-developments in human beings. There are forces in the inner life of human beings that also disappear, but then can come into view again in a changed form."

That lecture had brought Gerda great relief. She followed Rudolf Steiner's indications, and when she began her own teaching, she experienced how through Waldorf pedagogy the lost powers of fantasy do in fact return to work in a different way.

"Somewhere between the ninth and tenth year," she continued, "the child undergoes a remarkable change. The ninth year lies between the change of teeth and puberty. These two developments, manifesting as they do in bodily changes, are of course well-known. However, the event in the ninth year—'a transition in life,' Rudolf Steiner always called it—takes place primarily in the soul-and-spirit nature of the child.[1] But that doesn't mean it is therefore less significant. On the contrary, it has to do with a turning point in life of supreme importance: something now dries up, and something new appears."

This teacher, for whom I felt so deep a reverence, and from whom I had received such important indications, died at the age of seventy-three in 1970. I sensed her good spirit as a guiding star over this work from which I hope parents and teachers may draw some helpful ideas. I dedicate this book in great thankfulness to Gerda Langen.

Dornach, Michaelmas 1982

Part One

The Child in the Ninth Year

Conversation with Peter's Parents

Since the third grade had begun, more and more parents had been asking for a visit by the class-teacher: they wanted to know what was actually going on with their children.[1] The teacher set out on the first of such visits, and as he was walking along, he recalled how Peter had greeted him just that morning. He was a big lad with blue eyes, fair hair, and a couple of freckles on his nose. Once again he had met the teacher with his usual enthusiasm. The teacher had watched him entering the classroom. With each step, Peter seemed to "throw" his feet, as if his shoes were too heavy or too big for him, which was, however, not the case at all. Peter's way of walking showed he had some difficulty in connecting himself with the ground. His greeting was certainly spontaneous; recently, he had taken to shaking the teacher's hand with considerable vigor, yet at the same time letting his gaze glide slightly past the teacher. Only after the teacher had gently held on to his hand a few moments would Peter look him in the eye. Then he would run away to his friends, and carry on a loud and lively conversation with them. Like all children, these comrades of his had unsparingly taken note of his weaknesses and had nicknamed him "Face Twister" because of his occasional uncontrollable facial twitches. To this they added "Know-It-All" because he was given to making critical remarks, often voicing them pertly even during the lessons. And yet, despite this, Peter was a cheerful and straightforward boy.

Peter was the oldest child of the family and had two brothers and a sister. That evening at supper he was allowed to sit next to his teacher at the round table. He was immensely honored by this distinction, but he never said a word during the whole meal. When this was over, the children cleared the table. At a nod from their father, they said "Good night," and disappeared from the room. As soon as their mother had gone to do the dishes, Peter's father turned to the teacher and asked, "Why has my son suddenly become so critical?"

"I'll try to explain," said the teacher. "The criticism he shows has to do with his age. You will very often find this happening with the beginning of the ninth year. Until recently, your son was still lingering in his earlier imitative stage, simply acting out what was going on around him. In this childlike condition, he was still in something of a dream, in which he was, so to say, interwoven with his surroundings. Now, however, in this ninth year, that is all changed, for children at this time come to a kind of threshold in life. They wake up, and for the first time see what is around them far more consciously than ever before. They actually come to an inner change; they experience themselves, their own ego, much more deeply than before, and in consequence they look out into the world with newly observant eyes.[2] Moreover, they can follow the line of thought behind the events going on around them more clearly than was possible earlier on. Many things dawn on them that they had not been aware of at all before.

"This awakening can lead to a capacity for quiet wonder, but it can also lead to a tendency to criticize. The child now perceives more consciously behavior that strikes him as absurd and stupid; that his criticism frequently misses the mark is another matter. The ability to see connections between observations is not yet developed and must still be

4

acquired, and, of course, the child has not yet had the life-experience to be able to do this with any maturity. So, for instance, if his father has kept his outdoor shoes on although the children must always wear their slippers indoors, the child will consider this quite unfair. The father may have forgotten to take his shoes off, or he may also have to go out again soon and has left his shoes on as it was not raining, and they were not dirty. However, just this sort of thing is not usually taken into account by the child."

"Are you then saying," said the father, "that our Peter's inclination to criticize simply has to do with his age?"

"In a very real sense that is certainly so. At that age, children no longer see adults as inviolable or superior. Deep down he asks the question: How do adults come to know everything? And within this more or less unconscious query lurks the doubt whether they do in fact know everything. Boys come out more readily with their doubts and criticism at this age than girls, who are more inclined to withdraw and hold themselves back."

The teacher now remained silent. He asked himself whether in fact Peter's exceptional urge to criticize was only due to his age. The ninth year transition often brought something to the surface that was actually some kind of one-sidedness or weakness in the child's environment. Could that be so here? The teacher had noticed during the meal that the father's word on any topic, however spontaneous and unconsidered, was taken as final. His attitude set the tone for the family. His instructions were carried out at once by the children. It was as if all the time he were raising an invisible forefinger of paternal authority. Moreover, what he thus indicated always referred to something quite external. Any inner consideration seemed doomed to silence from the start. This was entirely understandable out of the family's circumstances, for with six hungry mouths to feed, making a living and managing the family was bound to be the focus of every day. Neither father nor mother had time for reading, and their only music was provided by the radio.

All this suddenly became clear to the teacher, and he had to ask himself if he could talk about it to the father, and point out that a child frequently reflects the characteristics of the adults around him. The teacher was anxious not to imply any kind of criticism. Yet the question of parental self-knowledge was important in the present situation.

Peter's father was already rejecting any critical utterances from his son. How then would he react if someone outside the family questioned any of his ways? The teacher realized that he depended fundamentally on the father's cooperation, but just at this point he could not muster either the courage or the words he needed. He found himself wondering how matters stood with his own self-knowledge, and how he himself would respond to such a criticism. But could he in all conscience just say nothing? Didn't he owe it to the child to be frank and open? Weren't the parents expecting some kind of answer from him? Wasn't his hesitation after all nothing but cowardice?

Just as he had pulled himself together and was about to say something, the father forestalled him and said with a smile, "Perhaps my son has adopted this know-all manner from myself. In my work, I have to supervise what other men are doing and, of course, occasions arise when I have to object to something or other. That could have left its mark on him, don't you think?"

The whole situation ended in laughter. The mother brought the tea things in from the kitchen; the teacher gave her a hand. Then while she was pouring the tea, he thought some more about the boy.

Peter's compulsive criticizing and also his tears—which despite his age could still come so readily into his eyes—did not both these things show that the boy was unable to withdraw into his own inner depths, his inner experience? The essential problem was how to nurture his soul-life. The teacher realized that he must take this question up quite directly. "Have you ever told Peter any stories," he asked the mother immediately. "I have tried to do just that," she answered with emphasis, "but I had no success at all, although I looked for the best fairy tales I could find. Peter flatly declared, 'I don't want fairy tales. I want to hear true stories.' The next day, at meal time, he made the remark, 'This table is not made of wood at all; it's only veneered.' This shows he wants to deal only with entirely real things. He wants nothing to do with fiction any more."

The teacher blamed himself for not having concerned himself with the family for so long; after all, it was more than two years ago since he had advised telling fairy tales to the boy. Since then many things had changed in Peter.

"Fairy tales are not the right thing for him any more," the teacher said, confirming the mother's opinion. "Your son has now crossed over the ninth-year threshold, and telling him fairy tales at this age would amount to holding him back artificially in his development. In fairy tales, little children live in a virtually paradisal union with the world, in which all things speak with and understand each other. After the transition in the ninth year, however, the child no longer experiences the world from inside, he no longer hears the secret whisperings between things, or apprehends how they reveal something inside themselves. The child now sees the world from outside, in all its mysterious silence. Questions awaken in the child; he wants to know the real world."

"Then are we not to tell him any more stories?" the mother asked. "Stories, most certainly, but no more fairy tales. What now interests your son are the connections between things in life itself, for example, what is happening on a farm. That would really interest him; or stories about life in the mountains or the forests, or what people are doing in their various places of work."

"But that would turn him to the outer world," the father objected, who until then had only been listening to the conversation. "The last time you were here you said, if I remember correctly, that our son should live a great deal in fantasy. In connection with this you spoke, I remember, of the inner world of the child."

"In a very real sense, the purpose of fairy tales," said the teacher, "is to prepare the child for the world; they are rather like the kind of dream one has just before waking up. Fairy tales help the child to see the world in its earthly reality, to recognize what is good or evil and useful or untrue in the world. Your boy, however, has moved on and is now in a quite different situation. For instance, when Peter is eating a piece of bread, he will now want to know all about baking, milling, harvesting, and so on."

"What should one do when children leave their bread crusts or even throw bread away?" the mother joined in quickly. "I find it dreadful. What would you do yourself?"

"Let us say we bake a loaf with a child," replied the teacher, "or even perhaps grind some grain in a little handmill, and then when out for a walk together we go past a grainfield where the crop is ripening. On such occasions one can talk to the child and tell him that the little grain is like a tiny loaf that the sun has baked. Also, that we, in our breadmaking, bring together the elements of water, air, and fire and so actually repeat what happens outside in nature through rain, wind, and the warmth of the sun. And so, when we are baking, we are doing something that goes on in creation, and this gives our work a special quality, a special mood."

"But when the child has no reverence for the bread, what is one to do then?" the mother said with a sigh.

"Consider how we produce the bread from the grain, how the grain ripens in the sunlight, and how the light is a force that lets everything grow and leads to the Creator. This is what nourishes us, the force at work in the bread. There is nothing of sentimental piety in this. This is a truth the child will experience if we say a verse such as this grace before we eat:

> From the grain the bread,
> From the light the grain.
> From the face of God
> The Light is born.
> The fruits of the Earth
> From out God's shine
> Bring light to birth too
> In this heart of mine.

"Once a child has experienced this, he will not throw any more bread away, or, if he does, he will believe it a just punishment if he doesn't get anything to eat at meal time."

"It seems to me," said the mother, after pondering this for a time, "that we do not concern ourselves enough with the considerations you have brought up. We two, as parents, have taken too little account of Peter's feelings, and he surely notices that. I remember that as a nine-year-old I once read in my reader a story entitled, 'The Hill Farmer.' The story spoke of autumn mists, of the cold, and of the snow that forced the farmer to stay inside his warm house. It told of the cozy cow barn and of the shepherds waiting behind the little windowpanes for spring to arrive. Then came the melting of the snow in the spring sunshine, the appearance of the first violets and primroses, the moving of the cattle to the mountain pastures, and still later the ascent of the farmer's men to the high meadows to make hay. One day, while I was still a child, a question came into my head. What is the farmer doing? He always follows the sun. When it sinks lower in winter, he goes indoors, and when it begins to climb higher in the sky, he, too, climbs to the heights. This is what I experienced at that time, and, as I became conscious of it, it was something quite special to me. And then one day, our teacher put just this question to me: 'What does the farmer do?' I remember well that I couldn't give an answer. I just couldn't put into words what I had so deeply experienced. And so it is, I'm sure, with our own child. A lot is going on inside him, even if he says nothing. We don't bother ourselves about it, and attach too little importance to what he leaves unsaid."

In the mother's emphasis on these last words— "importance" and "leaves unsaid"—her own inner concerns resonated. She sat silently, staring in front of her.

Now the father added, "When I was nine years old and in third grade, we read *Robinson Crusoe*. That was really something! We were soon building huts in the trees and fitting them out so we could live in them, and, well, we became regular Robinson Crusoes ourselves."

At this point it became clear to the teacher why Rudolf Steiner had advised against Daniel Defoe's *Robinson Crusoe* as a book for children.[3] If this book's picture of life were to implant itself in the young soul, the instinct for self-preservation would take on prime importance, and any trust in the spiritual guidance active in everyone's destiny would progressively diminish. And precisely this connection with the powers of destiny should not be lost, but if at all possible, it should be experienced in the ninth year.

Then, the teacher took up this theme, and said, "You know, I'm sure, that just now the children have been listening to the story of Joseph, and how he was sold away by his brothers, and how he was later able to help them. He was able to do this because of his honest, unegotistical character, but also because he had the help of the powers guiding his destiny. The part they played in this came to expression in his dreams. When a child believes such a story, it deepens his own relationship to a power greater than ourselves. He grows into a larger context, beyond his immediate surroundings.

"Something quite different is presented in *Robinson Crusoe*. Running through the whole narrative like a red thread, present everywhere though not explicit, is the question: How do I best help myself? It is all done in a very refined way and described with gripping power. It is dangerous, however, because it is one-sided. Everyone, of course, must look after himself to some extent, but he just couldn't exist if he didn't help others and they didn't help him. Now it is no different with Robinson Crusoe. Where did he get his musket, his powder, his axe, and his sword? If he hadn't had what the gunsmith, the blacksmith, and the carpenter had manufactured, he couldn't possibly have lived on his island. The social connection that is necessary in every person's life is just overlooked by Defoe in his story. This presents a danger for children if they try to live by it. After all, at this age, children want to live into their surroundings and their social connections in the widest sense; they want to get to know them."

"But there you are mistaken," protested the father. "It was precisely through building the tree house that we became a circle of sworn friends. What is more, we learned a great deal from it, from the carpenters and from other craftsmen. Our Robinson-life brought us together with lots of other people."

"You are right about that," said the wife in support of her husband. "What you were doing was just what you boys needed, and it was certainly a wonderful time for you. But just as surely there is another side to Crusoe. Everything with him is self-made. He anticipates the blasé self-made man of today. The story is really quite theoretical. As we all know, life often goes quite differently. Things can

11

happen as they did in Joseph's destiny, and only in the end does one see that there is a truly profound meaning in them. Perhaps this is what you had in mind," said the mother questioningly to the teacher.

"It is of course only a novel," the father conceded. "But I must say this, for boys—and for girls, too—at this age it is very good to work on something concrete and practical. After all, they must live in the real world later on, and the classroom is only one part of life. Their education can become quite one-sided if it isn't seen what life as a whole demands."

The teacher readily agreed. He knew only too well how great the danger was for learning to become abstract if the right connection and relationship with life were missing. Were the teacher to join with the children in nailing, sawing, building, plowing, and baking, it would help to set up a beautiful inner balance.

Peter was certainly a sloppy student, but how gladly he lent a hand and knuckled down to anything practical! Wouldn't he love the teacher much more if he were to work together with him? And moreover—that remained of course to be seen—wouldn't perhaps his written work begin to take on a different look?

At this point, the mother offered the teacher another cup of tea, but the teacher declined. He was a little at odds with himself. He wondered how he could bring what the father's observations had stirred in him into concrete actions.

"You know," the father said into the stillness, "the practical things in life are also very important. But I think one has to know where to begin and what would be the right timing. Just recently my son asked me how an electric current is produced. What sort of answer would you give?"

The teacher pondered for a moment. "He knows the dynamo on a bicycle. So one could say: 'Look, the current is produced by the bicycle wheel. How it works in detail you'll be learning in a few years' time. Now a small current is enough for a bicycle. Where one needs a much bigger current, a big wheel, or a turbine, is used and turned by waterpower.' Then one has to speak about waterpower, and in particular explain how the water that comes down from the mountains is dammed up. In this way, one gets back to the sun-forces, so that in the end the child has the feeling that these sun-forces, as in many other things, are within the current, only in a changed form. In any question connected with technical matters, one has to establish what the connection with nature is. There is nothing in technology that has not ultimately been derived from nature. Later on, of course, the child will be gradually familiarized with this sphere of technology. A start is made with physics in the sixth grade, but instruction in the sciences in the narrower sense cannot be fruitful until after the age of fourteen.

"But you are quite right. Many children these days are intensely interested in technical things at a very early age. Rudolf Steiner, himself the son of a railway employee, once said that it was the worst thing possible for a child to come to a mechanical understanding of how a locomotive or a tram works before the age of nine. It would be like driving a spike into his whole organization. It is something quite different to show a child how every technical achievement has somehow been slowly and arduously derived from nature.[4]

"With technology, we have added a fourth kingdom of nature to the other three, to the minerals, to the plants, and to the animals. These three—the mineral of course by way of the other two—are subject to the processes of life and decay, whereas everything technical is dead from the beginning."

"Naturally," agreed the father, "technology leads a sort of life of its own today. And that's why we have removed

13

ourselves farther and farther away from nature, which is to say that it's due to human beings, for without us there would be no technology at all to destroy life and the earth through its effects. We must go back. We must not get any farther away from nature, but rather discover her again. And that must also be taken into account in education. And so it is that a nine-year-old boy must first understand himself; he certainly doesn't learn to do that from technology, which is utterly dead and always threatens to draw humankind away from itself. We can see for ourselves in our children, for example, the bad effect television has on them."

"I think," said the mother, "that children should have a delight in the garden, a love for it, before they go into technical things. When we work together in the garden, how lovely that is, even when we are tired out in the evening! What a joy to look at a goldenrod with all its golden rain of blossom, or at the young green of the birch, or again the splendid clouds of spring as they sail across the vast blue of the sky. Yesterday I recalled a Psalm I had learned as a child:

> Praise the Lord, O my soul:
> O Lord my God, thou art very great:
> Thou art clothed with honor and majesty.
> Who coverest thyself with Light as with a garment:
> Who stretchest out the heavens like a curtain:
> Who layest the beams of His chambers in the waters:
> Who maketh the clouds His chariot:
> Who walketh upon the wings of the wind.
>
> (Ps. 104)

"When I was a child these words didn't say very much to me, but now they have quite a different meaning. This Psalm of David is a real force of the heart, and so the children should also learn something of this kind for their later life."

"We must go on a little more about Peter," the father now said. "His urge to criticize, I see more clearly now what it is connected with. A part of it he has from me, but then I'm sure he also needs something that will inwardly fill him more. He is not yet fully at home within himself. Do you see what I mean?"

"Yes, indeed I do," said the teacher. "I entirely agree with you. At school, I'll try to win more of his interest, but the nine-year-old is helped through his difficulties in a quite special way when the parents talk with him—talk with him, that is, about other things apart from the daily events. The thoughts that the father and mother arrive at together can make a very strong impact on the child. The lack of balance in the child can be corrected by the harmony between father and mother. Children always experience this as a blessing, but especially so at this turning point in the ninth year.

"Then let us hope that the talk we have had today will be a further help. I have often experienced that it's of direct benefit to a child when adults make time to consider what is just as essential for the child to live as food and drink are. The best thing would be if we could meet again in the near future."

On his way home later that night, the teacher felt closer to Peter's parents. He had seen that they had also applied that stern measure of self-education to themselves, which he as a teacher knew only too well to be the necessary precondition for an educator. This understanding produced a strong feeling of inner closeness to the parents. And so, despite many difficulties, he arrived at a much better relationship with Peter. And just that is of the greatest possible importance in the phase of transition in the ninth year.

Some time later, prompted by what Peter's father had said, the teacher built a little wooden house with his class. When it was almost finished, the children begged the teacher to make a door for it, otherwise one would not be able to shut out the world and be alone in the house. This was no easy task for the teacher with his limited carpentry skills, but along came Peter's father to help hang the door with a very sure hand. "Our tree house also had a door," he said and grinned. "It hung on leather hinges. Incidentally, my wife sends you her greetings. She urged me to tell you that since your last visit, Peter has been quite different. And I think so too. Or maybe we see him differently— perhaps a little bit of both. Anyway, one thing is quite certain: Something has awakened in him that was entirely hidden before."

Conversation with Monica's Parents

The last notes of the music were fading away. While Monica's mother was putting her daughter to bed, her father stayed behind in the music room with the teacher and took the opportunity to pour out his heart to him. "We are very glad you have come to see us this evening," he said. "For, quite frankly, we are very worried about Monica. As you yourself know, she is a sensitive and very gifted child, at least where music is concerned, and now we are noticing things about her, especially just recently, that really disturb us. It is not just a passing mood or temporary change. My wife has observed the most extraordinary happenings."

Meanwhile the mother had come back into the room again, and now said, "You would have seen the best example of this just now. She has fallen into the strangest habits. She won't lie down to sleep until she has first looked under the bed to see if anyone is there; she has just repeated this nightly ritual. Then she carefully pulls back the blanket, as if some stranger might be lying there in her bed."

"Isn't that extraordinary?" asked the father. "Something or other must surely be going on inside her."

"But that isn't the only thing," continued the mother. "In the hallway, there is a big mirror. It hangs near a wardrobe. It is difficult to believe, but there are times when Monica will almost not walk past that mirror. A day or two ago, I had to stand in front of it before she would go into the music room, which is opposite the mirror on the other side of the hallway."

"My wife is quite proud of the fact that she could hide the whole mirror," Monica's father said jokingly. Warding off his wife's gentle attacks at this with a smile, the husband continued, "We have now hung coats over the mirror, so that at any rate it won't trouble our daughter any more." The teacher was listening to all this with full attention. "But that isn't all," the mother continued. "I must tell you something else I saw a little while ago." The father interrupted. "My wife was standing at the second floor window. It overlooks the whole street. Along came Monica from school; she was dawdling a little, as she usually does. Suddenly, however, she began running as if she had gone crazy, running as if someone, I don't know who, were after her."

"But there was no one at all to be seen, not a soul in the whole street," the mother interjected. "She ran up to the front door, fumbled in a great hurry for her key, and then she scarcely found the keyhole. Finally, Monica opened the door, jumped on the doormat, and, what did she do then? What did she do then? You tell, you saw and heard what she did," Monica's mother said as she nodded to her husband.

"First she stamped with her feet, and then she muttered softly to herself, 'Saved, saved.' Do you find that quite normal?" The father looked at the teacher expectantly.

For a while the teacher considered what he had heard without speaking. Then he said, "I can't give an explanation in the usual sense. However, it may perhaps help you to know that it isn't only you who are worried by experiences of this kind—experiences with children who, like your own daughter, are having to cope with the transition between the ninth and tenth year."

"Please, tell us more about that," said the father.

18

"At this age, the child stands at an actual threshold, the threshold between early childhood and the entirely new impressions that meet the child now. The child suddenly takes notice of her environment, whereas previously this wasn't the case at all; one might almost say she had been enjoying what was around her in a kind of sweet dreaming, through imitating the adults. That is over now, and Monica senses this. Everything you have described is in some way connected with this. But what I would really like to say is not the kind of scientific explanation people ask for these days."

"Don't worry about that," said the father. "Do go on!"

"In a way," said the teacher with a smile, "it's like dream interpretation, and so there are various possibilities one can think of. I believe that in all you have observed one thing stands out clearly over and over again: Your daughter is experiencing the transition I have mentioned in a special way—whether in connection with the actual threshold of the house or the transition from day to night; one can see that without any difficulty."

"And the mirror?" asked the mother.

The teacher considered this for a moment. "As I have already said, you are not alone in these experiences. The mirror is one of the things in the home that the child has to come to terms with."

"But why?" asked the mother.

"One can't explain it, or rather, I don't know of any explanation. But one can inwardly follow what is going on in a child's soul when it is disturbed by her own reflection. Monica doesn't want the meeting with herself in this external way. It is just at this time that her ego first lays hold of her destiny. In this threshold-situation, she experiences herself, and for the child's feeling the mirror reflection is a caricature, and this she shrinks away from."

19

"I had no idea at all," said the mother, "that such a thing as that was behind all this." She pondered in silence. "But if this is something to do with the age of the child," objected the father, "other children must also have such experiences. Do you know of any?"

"I certainly do," the teacher said in agreement. "Only one must take into account that children are very different from one another. What you have observed in your own child is actually not all that unusual. At most what is unusual is the intensity, the strength of feeling, the degree of excitement with which everything emerges in Monica's case."

"But have other children really the same sort of experiences?" demanded the father, pressing the teacher further. The mother, however, interrupted him here with another line of thought.

"I have just remembered how deeply our daughter has been impressed lately by all that you have been saying in class. I see it in her immediately. She turns it over in her mind. Your account of the Fall of Man haunted her. Again and again she has come to me, asking what evil really is, where it comes from, and why God allows it. She presses me hard with many questions. But actually what I say in answer she doesn't take much notice of at all. She only wants to speak to someone about it, and then she pursues the matter further on her own."

"When I was telling the story of the Fall," the teacher said, "everyone in the classroom was as quiet as a mouse. The children listened with the closest attention. You could have heard a pin drop. As you have observed, at this stage in their life children are much concerned with good and evil.

"I don't want to bypass your question," the teacher said to the father, "but in a way everything is connected. Just today a former colleague, now seventy years old and no longer able to cope with a lot of writing, was dictating her memoirs to me. What I wrote down I have here in my briefcase, and I'd like to read the passage to you where she describes her experiences when she was nine years old: 'In that year, I had a significant ego-experience. I was coming from a lesson in the town and had to change streetcars. I was waiting at the trolley stop, and at that very moment it dawned on me with absolute certainty that ahead of me there lay my whole life and that it was I myself who would have to lead it. It became equally clear to me that from then on there would be things I would have to carry through entirely on my own. And it was just as certain to me that I would have to contend with evil.' "

Folding the paper again, the teacher said, "You see that nine-year-olds took this same step in development then as now. And furthermore, I don't know whether you noticed that the scenery, so to speak, at the trolley stop corresponded to some extent to the description of your daughter's threshold-experience. In most cases, people don't observe their children as closely as you have done. Nor is it so often seen what decisive turns in life are being prepared for in the depths of the child's soul."

"It's as if something quite new wants to enter into Monica, but just can't manage to do so. What is actually happening?" There was a certain uneasiness in the father's voice.

"Yes, you are right. And," said the teacher, "it is the ego-being of the child that is trying to enter. That is one thing that is too little noticed and unfortunately far too little supported. The other is that the beautiful childhood-world has to be left behind; it sinks out of sight. Fear then arises in the child. Just listen to what I have here. It is a poem I was allowed to copy out of the poetry album my old colleague had kept from her childhood. She wrote the poem when she was nine years of age."

Into the sea the sun sinks, glowing red:
No smallest winds astir, all things are hushed:
Now is the sun half-sunk within the sea:
In the heavens are little sparklets, still a-glowing:
Now is the sun quite sunk beneath the sea:
In the heavens, the last small sparks have died away
And round me everything is drear and empty,
As if the sun I'd never see again.

The teacher looked at the parents with an observant eye. The mother was looking down, as if she were trying to remember something from her own past. The father appeared deeply impressed, and it seemed as if he wanted to say something, but couldn't find the words. Finally, the teacher broke the silence and asked, "What did you experience when you were nine or ten years old?"

"I've been trying all the time to remember," said the mother, "and now I know for sure. It was then that I lost my father." Then she fell silent again.

Her husband looked at her sympathetically, then suddenly said, "You know, my memory of that time is quite similar; it is also connected with death. On my ninth birthday, my parents promised me that we would go to the seaside for the summer vacation. I was born in spring, so I was nine years and about four months when the vacation came to which I had so looked forward, and we went to a small island. What I experienced there one day still stands clearly before me. I was standing with my father among a crowd of people who were quite silent. There came past us a group of sailors who were carrying a very heavy iron coffin; they laid it down in a boat. Then, they rowed out into the open sea so far that at last I could hardly make out the boat. Then my father said, 'Look, they are lowering the coffin into the water. The captain is to find his last resting-place at the bottom of the sea.' I shall never forget the impression this made on me. Never before had it entered my mind a man could lie one day in a coffin."

The father lapsed into deep thought. Something was going on inside him that unsettled him. It was with sympathy that the teacher looked at him.

"You said earlier," the father continued hesitantly and in an unexpectedly very deep voice, "that your explanation could be compared to the interpretation of a dream, and that would leave other possibilities open." Obviously inwardly agitated, the father looked intently into the eyes of the teacher. "Who is this unknown being my daughter looks for under the bed; who does she suddenly feel is near her and from whom is she fleeing into the house? Who is it? Could it not just as well be something or someone good?"

"You mustn't get so worked up," said the wife, trying to calm him down. "My husband and I, you should know, have been suspecting something extraordinary, but after what you have told us this evening our anxiety seems quite groundless. Don't you think so too?" She said this to her husband, seeking again to allay his agitation.

"I must tell you straight out," the father said. "We have got the impression that our daughter has intimations of death of a quite definite kind, a feeling that she will soon be leaving us. With so highly sensitive a child, such a premonition would surely be quite possible." It was obvious that this was why the father had been so urgent in asking the teacher to visit.

"As far as that is concerned, I can really set your minds at rest. What you have observed tallies with what other parents have also noticed in their children at this stage of transition. Your observations are quite correct, but you were coming to a different conclusion which, if I may say so, was quite incorrect." The father quickly glanced at the teacher.

"I don't quite see what you mean about observation and conclusion," said the mother.

"In a way you were quite right in what you felt. When the expulsion from Paradise took place, as I said earlier on, these words were spoken: 'Dust you are, and to dust you shall return.' But that didn't mean that Adam and Eve were to die there and then. Something different was being expressed. An element now enters the child's consciousness that wasn't there before, and that is awareness of human mortality."

"You yourself heard our Monica at the piano this evening. She makes up the words of her songs herself, and they always have to do with death. I wonder if what you have been saying can explain such an early ripening of artistic talent." The father looked down at the carpet with a set expression.

"What moved me especially when your daughter was playing," said the teacher reassuringly, "was the thought that here is a child of only nine years who already begins to give pain and death an artistic form. It really fascinates me when a young child attempts this. Only a few children could achieve this at nine years old although all children go through this painful experience, but your daughter is freeing herself from it by giving it form. I could see this as she left the piano. As an artist yourself, I am sure you are quite familiar with this process." The two men looked quietly at each other for a moment.

"Perhaps I could add something rather personal to what I have been saying," said the teacher with some hesitation. The father meanwhile had recovered his composure. "When you go too far with your questioning, your child will withdraw still further into herself. She is then focusing on herself too much and experiences a depressing mood. Let her just go ahead and make music as she pleases, without your seeing anything unusual in it. You'll soon see that her music is a kind of self-healing for her."

"Maybe you are right. I see I have in fact been misinterpreting her elegiac-melancholic way of expressing her loss of childhood's paradise. It seems that we have only to do, so to say, with death's imprint, not with death itself. I will live with this view of yours; I am glad to have heard it."

While they were speaking, the father had risen and fetched the Bible. He wanted to read the Book of Genesis. The teacher stood up to leave.

"Please, do stay a little longer," begged the mother. "You have given us some real help already this evening, but there is something else that also troubles me. Perhaps, you can help us in this as well. You had the impression that our daughter went away from the piano in an easier and freer mood. It may be as you say, but I experienced something quite different." Hesitating for a moment, she then continued, "Previously, I could be together with my daughter at the piano, or she would come and say, 'Mommy, do come. I want to play something for you.' How her eyes would shine just then! We were one heart and soul together. But now it disturbs her if I am simply there in the room. And do you think she ever asks me now if she can play something for me? She doesn't think of it. She plays for hours for herself—for herself alone. Then she gets up as if deeply satisfied, just as you said, but then goes into the garden or visits a friend or does some homework. She does everything, that is, but come to me. It's as if something had come between us. It's been like that ever since she began third grade. Often I think I am losing my child; she is no longer at my side."

"This morning," said the teacher, "I was telling the children about the sacrificing of Isaac. I must confess that for the longest time I myself could not understand this story. Through what you have just told me, however, I

.

begin to see for the first time something of its deeper meaning."

The mother was listening with the closest attention.

"For a long time," continued the teacher, "I couldn't see what meaning there could be in testing whether Abraham loved God or his own son more. Now, however, I realize what the difference is. Love for God shows itself when we glimpse the working of a higher, divine power in the necessary developmental phases a child undergoes, and help this higher will, this necessary development to fully take effect. And this, even if, as in this transition phase, it requires the sacrifice that the love of the mother become so great that it lets the child go free. Something essential would not be able to enter into the child, or at any rate it would be made more difficult, if the will to let the child go were not present in the parents."

The teacher paused. The mother seemed to understand him, and yet something in her rejected his interpretation. "That is surely the problem of father and son."

"Up to a point that could also be true," said the teacher, "but the story of the sacrifice of Isaac is taken further in Jewish legends. As the story continues, Satan goes to Sarah in the guise of an old man and says to her, 'Do you know what has happened? At God's command Abraham has sacrificed your son Isaac. The boy wept and begged for mercy, but his father showed him none.' Sarah let out a bitter cry, tore her clothes, and threw herself on the ground. Weeping, she said, 'Isaac, Isaac, my son! I was ninety years old when I bore thee, and now thou hast been given up to the knife and the fire. But it was what God commanded,' she said, 'and what He does is right. It is only my eyes that weep; my heart rejoices.'

Sarah had no peace and went seeking Abraham, but although she sought him everywhere, she could not find him. Then the devil changed into a younger man, and coming to her said, 'Isaac lives. Abraham has not sacrificed him.' At these words, Sarah was taken with such joy that her heart broke, and she sank down to the ground, dead." The teacher saw that the mother was experiencing a tremendous inner struggle. He would gladly have said something to help her, but an inner voice told him to hold his peace. The mother said nothing.

Finally, the father broke the silence; he had found the account of Isaac's sacrifice in the Bible and had quickly read it. Looking up, he saw how it was with his wife, and he began to read:

Because thou hast done this thing and hast not withheld thy son, thine only son, in blessing I will bless thee and in multiplying I will multiply thy seed as the stars of the heaven, and as the sand which is upon the seashore, and in thy seed shall all the nations of the earth be blessed.

"That is pointing to the birth of Christ." said the teacher.

The mother was as if transformed. She turned to her husband and said, "I think that for the first time I have an understanding of deeper relationships. Christ is the bringer of neighborly love, and that is not family love, blood-love. That is why my daughter must turn away from me. But I now see that a new being is seeking to enter into her: her own being, and this wants to be free of the older love, the mother-love. But she will love her mother again one day. We have had something quite untrue in mind. We have been grieving for the past. Like a reflection in the waves of a lake, the traits of childhood scatter and vanish; they are over and gone. Now for the first time our child comes truly to herself. We are blessed to be near her and be allowed to experience all this with our daughter. I am altogether happy about it. I see her now with quite different eyes."

27

Dear Parents

This evening we are gathered again to consider the important step in development that your children are going through now between the ages of nine and ten. Rudolf Steiner said: "In the ninth year the child actually experiences a total transformation of his being, which points to a significant transformation of his soul-life and to a significant transformation of his experience of the bodily-physical."[1]

What kind of transition is this?

Until now, your children have been living—some more, some already less so—in the so-called age of imitation. Put yourself for a moment as fully as you can into the place of the little child. If you did this, then when I put my finger on my mouth, you would all do the same. And if I then said a little rhyme like: "Pease pudding hot, pease pudding cold," you would all automatically say it after me. And when I put my finger on my mouth again, all would be quiet once more.

After all, it was through imitation that the child learned to speak. Imagine that for some reason a four- or five-year-old child came to a place where only Chinese is spoken. In a few months, the child would already be speaking Chinese. However, it would be a long time before we adults could speak this language. We can see from this that the power of imitation is like a stream in which the child is immersed and through which the child takes in and learns an extraordinary amount from his or her surroundings.

As long as this imitative capacity is present, children are quite incapable of experiencing aloneness; they are one with the world. During the ninth year, however, this changes, and for the first time children feel themselves to be quite on their own in the world. Their earlier ability to feel so self-evidently and naturally a part of everything is no more; it has disappeared in a mysterious way together with the faculty of imitation.

We can observe that children have now become strangers. We have already seen something like this happen. When they are about two-and-a-half years old, for example, and someone comes into their bedroom, they turn around very quickly, or they pull the bedclothes over their head. That was the time when the child used the word "I" for the first time, a process that now, seven years later, is repeated on a far deeper level. Children now seem to shut out their parents, teachers, brothers, sisters, and even their peers. To recognize this, one must certainly observe the children with great sensitivity. They withdraw into themselves, but they actually want to experience the opposite. They carry within themselves the unspoken question: "Do you still love me?" They will often approach us on some pretext or other, but what they are really longing for is to experience again our love through a good, warm-hearted word.[2]

Before the ninth year, we did not meet with this attitude in our children. It is connected with the sense of separation, with the loss of the imitative capacity, and with the inability to connect again but now in an entirely new way with the environment. What goes on in the young human soul at this time of transition speaks to us in the following lines of a nine-year-old girl. She listed ten questions and then added one more:

1. Why must I live?
2. Why do I go on a trip?

30

3. Why do I have to go to school?
4. Why should I be nice to you?
5. Why do I need a bed?
6. Why do I have to have feet?
7. Why can I be mean?
8. Why do I have to write?
9. Why do I have to be pretty?
10. Why can I be me?

And finally she scribbled next to this little self-portrait: "Why does it always begin with 'why'?"

Fundamentally, every child follows this path through the crisis of aloneness. We notice it particularly in the child's eyes. We no longer see the merry, roving, starlike eyes, but rather a look that is much steadier and tinged with a touch of melancholy. Nightmares can occur at this age, and the children often complain about physical symptoms, such as headaches and stomach-aches. Thus, you can see that the child experiences an absolute crisis. But in this crisis, the child comes to experience that he or she bears an *I* within. No one can say this word to the child from the outside: the feeling must arise entirely from within.

How can we help children to come to this ego-discovery in the right way? Here again we find the greatest help of all in the curriculum developed by Rudolf Steiner. When we teach children according to this curriculum, we help them to process, that is, to awaken and to master in their life and learning precisely what corresponds to the stage of development to which their age has brought them. Let me give you a concrete example.

You know, of course, that at the beginning of the third grade we have discussed the story of Genesis from the Old Testament. First of all, we asked the question, "What would not be in the world if we thought away everything human beings have made?" This included houses, streets, cars, mopeds, the school, the Bible, pictures, arithmetic, writing, and a great deal more. Many things vanished before our eyes in our classroom. But what would be left? What would be left in our classroom that is not man-made? There would be the teacher, the children, the air, the light, the flowers, love, and the water in the tap. Then, we took up the question, What would vanish if we thought away all that God had created? The answer: We would no longer have trees, air, light, sun, stars, moon, and the whole earth. After we had experienced this strongly, the children closed their eyes and tried to hear where all these things had been before God created them. It was quite still in the classroom. After a while, a few came and whispered their answers into the teacher's ear. "With God," said some; "In God's heart," said others, or "In Heaven." Only one child said, "Nowhere."

The next day we began with the story of the Creation. "In the beginning God created the Heaven and the earth. And the earth was without form and void; and darkness was upon the face of the deep. And the Spirit of God moved upon the face of the waters. And God said, Let there be light."

And now there was light in the eyes of the children. They could experience that within themselves a light can be kindled and that then the world is also illuminated radiantly.

Then we tried to express these divine words "Let there be light" through painting with watercolors. Even before the children dipped their brushes into the dishes filled with yellow paint, a brief conversation started. First of all, we asked, "How can we experience that the light comes from God? Where is the light in us?" The children said, "In our paint dishes there is only yellow paint. We can make this color shine or not. We can paint yellow in a thick coat that is evenly yellow all over. Or we can paint it so that it is very thin in some places and yet shines out strongly. When we paint the light like this, so that there really is light in our

32

pictures, then the power of God is also working through us. Painting is therefore something sacred. Through the colors we listen to the power of God in our hearts." This is approximately what the children experienced and said.

For the first time since they had been going to school, the children then painted the yellow so that the color could really shine out. And one of the most beautiful moments of that lesson was to see that even the child who had earlier answered the question about where all things had been prior to being created with "nowhere" was able to paint a wonderful picture.

Then we came to the creation of humankind. The children heard that only after He had created the entire outer world did God create human beings. They heard how the angels brought to Him everything they could find in nature. He transformed what they brought and thus formed a human being. They brought Him the solid stone. What did God make out of that? A flurry of alternating questions and answers started. What did He make out of the stones? The bones. What out of the earth? The flesh. What out of the waves? The blood, tears, and saliva. What out of the wind? The breath. What out of the sun? The heart.

We came up with a lot of things. "But something is still lacking, something that human beings harbor within themselves as the most precious treasure, and which God could not take from outer nature and transform."

God the Father crowned His creation in that He gave human beings something of Himself: a breath from His own divine breathing.

> Adam, the living breath essay
> I give thee with this light of day.[3]

As the warm breath-stream of God ensouls Adam's breast, the earth- colored sheath that cloaks him falls away.

33

With deep breaths, he begins to awaken to the immensity of what has happened.

What is this experience of Adam that now also touches the souls of the children? They begin to have an inkling that the world spread out before them conceals a great mystery. They hear God's breath in the wind, hear His voice in the thunder, feel His great soul in the vast blue expanse of the sky. They begin to have a subtle feeling that their life, too, is of divine origin. The child's soul sings in jubilation when it becomes aware that all of nature is God's creation: the chirping birds, the pattering raindrops, and the skipping lambs.

The children also experience their own body in quite a new way, as formed by God and as a gift from God. Yes, indeed, and what a wonderful gift the feet now are, which carry the children into the world, and the hands, with which they can do so many things! And inwardly the children feel something special, something that connects them with God. A profound sense of gratitude fills their young hearts.

Here is how one child expressed these experiences in a psalm:

Thanks, Lord,
that I can breathe, that I can live.
That I can see how the little lambs skip,
how the little birds twitter, how the rain patters down,
how the water spurtles forth . . .
Thanks, that I can speak
when you ask a question . . .
That you have given me ears so that I can hear
when you speak to me . . .
That I can walk when I want to go out
or when we children play catch with each other.
Thanks, that you have given me arms and I
can receive you or when I am to fetch something . . .

We thank you for the golden ears of grain that nourish
us.
What light is the eternal light?
What does the Lord in Heaven consist of?
I believe out of the eternal light
the Lord gives to each one
a little spark of the eternal light . . .
for all this I thank you, Lord.

Do you remember, dear parents, the questions of the
nine-year-old girl and the agony of soul that could be heard
in them? And here, in contrast, you can hear the wonderful
warm joy streaming out of the human heart after the child
at this turning point has been imbued through and through
with soul life.

We could be tempted to close our parents' meeting at this
point; for by now we have seen the extraordinary
development taking place in the children. We have seen the
"significant transformation of soul life, the crucial change
in bodily-physical experience" that has been accomplished.

However, the *Paradise Play* does not end with these
primeval images of our creation; there is a tremendously
important task hidden in the further course of the play.
While Adam is still in his earth-colored sheath, the devil
creeps up with a surly face. He doesn't like it at all that
Adam is not to remain a creature of nature, but is to be
allowed to rise up to the freedom of creative spirits.
Nevertheless, the Evil One carries the sheath off triumphantly,
as if to say "I'll just find another way to spoil human
development, and I shall certainly succeed!"

This is then represented, as you know, through the Fall
of Man. Now the Fall, with its swiftly changing moods
from right to wrong and to the breach of God's commandment can actually be fully experienced by the children only
around the twelfth year when they come into the pre-
puberty phase. The "insertion" of the ego in the ninth year

inaugurates this process, giving the ego from now on the possibility to become completely separate from its origin.[4]

Let us now turn our attention for a moment to the figure of God the Father. What does He embody? How can we grasp Him with our small human dimensions, and above all what does He have to say to us as educators?

I believe, dear parents, that you will agree with me in seeing in this creator-figure in part an embodiment of the principle of authority. God creates human beings and cares for them. He punishes them for breaking His commandment, and sends Adam and Eve out into the world—into freedom. He acknowledges and respects the individual experience that has been gained through disobedience and looks into the future with confidence in the creative power in human beings. The concluding words of the *Paradise Play* give expression to this:

> But see, what wealth this Adam hath won:
> Like to a god he is become.
> Knowledge he hath of evil and good:
> He can lift up his hand on high,
> Whereby he liveth eternally.

Dear parents, from this point of view the Creator embodies what you mean to your child. You, too, have led the child into existence, have cared for him or her and given the child all that he or she needs. You lead the child into life, and, particularly in the second seven years, you also encounter conflicts. Then, at about age fourteen, the child enters the third seven-year period. At this time, you release your child into freedom, knowing that experience is possible only through a "fall into sin." You also know that the power for proper development of freedom has been implanted in your child through your educational efforts during the years of authority.

Rudolf Steiner established the principle of authority as the guideline for the second seven years. After the ninth year, "the mere principle of imitation can no longer work; another principle must now enter. That is the principle of authority. If I don't stand before the child between his seventh and fourteenth or fifteenth year as an authority, it is the same for his soul-spirit nature as it would be for his physical body if I were to cut off two of his fingers or his arm."[5]

In this connection, let us take a concrete example. Let us say your son has stolen some money and has bought cigarettes. You have, of course, "smelled" something wrong and found out what has happened. You are justifiably angry and indignant. But what's to be done? In the first place, you must connect with your child, and that can't be done with annoyance and anger, understandable as they may be under the circumstances. Instead, you need to ask: Are there perhaps difficulties occurring in the immediate relationships of the child that are inwardly related to what he has done? That may be so or not. It is good, however, in just such a situation to look at our own mistakes and weaknesses. That is painful; sometimes this leads parents to back away from doing anything further in the matter. Yet, we must not let ourselves be paralyzed by this experience. Is the confrontation with our own failings after all only painful? Inasmuch as we try to know ourselves, failings included, don't we come a little nearer to our own true being? In reality, the recognition of one's limitations releases the soul from the spell and bondage of past mistakes. Our soul is now for the first time free for forceful action.

And now there comes a conversation between father, mother, and son. (The archetype of authority, God the Father, is represented on earth by both father and mother.) Only when father and mother in inner accord with each other speak with the child do they have true authority. If the parents are separated and a conversation together isn't possible, then perhaps a godparent or one of the teachers can be included. In any case, it is good if two adults are present.

Then, you can ask the child to tell what he did—just as you have described your own imperfections to yourselves. Then you can express to the child your sorrow about what he has done.

And now, as the conversation proceeds, you come to a door through which the child can go only hand-in-hand with the adults. The child can't go alone for the door opens into that soul region where the adult, because of having been honest with himself, can find the power to transform darkness into light.

The parents are in fullest sympathy with their son. It is out of this feeling and united with him that they speak to him: They tell him how much they hope that it will again be bright in his heart. The inner strength for this hope the parents have built up for themselves beforehand, and now they express it also for their child. Through this the child is able to experience how deeply his parents care for him. Such a conversation can be compared with a pair of scales, whose pans gradually find their balance.

Of course, the parents must also speak with the child about replacing the money. The child himself can use his imagination and make suggestions for what he should do. Such details can be handled in different ways.

What is more important, however, is that through the authoritative guidance of father and mother the child learns how a problem of the soul can be solved. That cannot be achieved through any severe instantaneous punishment, for that would later on lead to what is termed "repression." And that unfortunately is what often does come about, especially when a parent is absent in the child's upbringing, or when the father and mother do not share the raising of the child.

If the parents with the child at their hands between them go from time to time through the door that leads into this holy, inner region of the soul, where through the force of truth we make peace with ourselves, then the child will be prepared for the great problems of life.

A great deal is said today about mastering psychological problems, and that is something that will become ever more important and increasingly fewer people will be able to manage. However, if parents lead their child in the way I have described, then a power of the soul will unfold as the child grows. And when the young person will have to withstand severe inner tensions later on, he or she will be more able—as we hope with all our hearts—to solve his or her difficulties.

There have been parents, too, who have confided in me that such conversations with their child have become something that they would not have wanted to miss on any account. The mood that can develop during such talks can recall what we read in the Gospel of Matthew: "For where two or three are gathered together in my name, there am I in the midst of them." (Matthew 18:20)

In this way, the parents can become the supporting and also the beloved authority for the child. I am aware that this requires an extra inner readiness and possibly even an overcoming of our own weaknesses, but that is only all to the good.

From the ninth and tenth year on, children cannot and should not be educated any longer by imitation. It is necessary that from now on in the child there develops an inner voice and the parents and teachers should strengthen it. Children cannot bring this about on their own; they need the guidance of authority.

Dear parents, this evening we have seen how our children now go through a very special process of development. If they are to find their way properly in life later on, if they are to find their life's task, then a basic precondition for that must be prepared at this very time. Christian Morgenstern wrote a poem that gives expression to what can become in adult life of what each human being may take in as a seed during the transition-time around the age of nine or ten.

> Creature no more, thoughts fully in his power:
> Will's lord, a slave no more beneath its sway:
> Master of feeling, measuring it aright:
>
> Too deep, to sicken in denial sour:
> Too free, for stubbornness in him to stay:
> Thus with the Spirit-realm does man unite,
>
> Thus to the Throne of Thrones he finds his way.[6]

The Ninth Year in Biography

The biographies of outstanding personalities can teach us a great deal about the transition in the ninth year. We can see how just at this time the individual's central life-motif, as it were, comes to the fore. Rudolf Steiner is said to have told Walter Johannes Stein at one time that in the ninth year of life, each person meets a human being whose image is indelibly inscribed in his or her soul.[1]

This is the case, for example, with Heinrich Schliemann (1822-1890), the German archaeologist who discovered the ruins of Troy. When he was nine years old, he and his friend Minna, who was the same age and lived on the neighboring farm, made an extraordinary resolution. They decided to marry when they were older and together they would then unearth Troy and the royal graves of Mycenae. After the children had pledged themselves to what proved to be the leitmotif of Schliemann's whole life, they were forever separated by all-decisive outer events. Only the resolution Heinrich had sworn to with Minna survived this loss of the nine-year-old Heinrich victoriously—a loss the archaeologist never forgot as long as he lived.

> I thank God that throughout all the twists and turns of my eventful life my firm belief in the existence of that Troy never left me! But only in the autumn of my life, and then without Minna—and far, far away from her— was I allowed to carry out our childhood dreams of fifty years before.[2]

***

The poet and doctor Hans Carossa (1878-1956) recalled experiences he had between his ninth and tenth year:

> Thus, the fever-loosened soul found itself swept this way and that between all and nothing in an extraordinary way. . . . All at once, the boy was longing for a figure, perhaps a companion, perhaps a leader or a misleader; it was neither man nor woman he had in mind, but it must be a being that would open up for him a life incomparably mightier than before, and he was ready to take on great suffering for its sake.[3]

Blurred, but all the same recognizable, the features of the Healer are dimly glimpsed by the boy. Rudolf Steiner spoke of the mystery of the healing force:

> We can experience the illness and our helplessness, and we can experience the Savior, the healing force, when we experience the helplessness, when we have connected ourselves with death in our soul. When we become aware of the Healer, we feel that we bear something in our soul that can at all times rise from the dead in our own inner experience.[4]

This is what the poet-doctor who was healing through the word had already glimpsed in his childhood. The young Carossa was visited by a playmate, a girl who was a little older than he; her ninth year experience was already behind her.

> Then, at last, there came Eva, bringing snowdrops and urging me to get up. She had become tall, pale, and womanly, and it took some time for me to relate to her as I had before. She kept sighing, and then would begin to turn round and round in the room with delightful dancing movements; the walls seemed to resonate and, when she had finished, to quiver for several seconds.

When I began to show off a bit with Latin and talk of my future doings in the town, she listened quietly. She then confided that she had also been in Kading for the longest time, and that a brother of her dead mother had visited her, who wanted to take her off to Munich and have her trained as an equestrian artist. She would get a white horse to ride on and a blue-green silk dress covered with lots of tiny mirrors.

But she didn't want anything of that at all; she wanted to become a dancer. "And I will have my way," she said.

"And yet," I put in, "you always used to want to ride."

"As a child I often longed to be a white horse, and later on I wanted to ride on one. But now I intend to dance." With this she began again to dance around the room, lightly and confidently. I looked on quite enchanted; the last traces of dejection disappeared, and, for the first time, a feeling of renewed health permeated all my limbs.[5]

***

The Austrian painter Oskar Kokoschka (1886-1980) experienced his life-transition in the face of death, which dominated his thoughts and paralyzed his will. The old storyteller, who had lived near Oskar's home, had died. Kokoschka writes about this as follows:

> I couldn't really understand what it meant to be dead. The only thing I realized was that she had disappeared and remained so. I can't just disappear like that, I thought to myself. Of course, she isn't here, but she must be somewhere.

The next morning Oskar sees the hearse in the street, and a white box is lying inside.

For a long time I gazed at the strange carriage. Its departure reminded me of an earlier experience, when I had seen such a vehicle for the first time. Dimly I began to glimpse the fact that the outer world after all had its boundaries too. It was an experience of the irretrievable, and this I felt as a transition from the light of day to the thoughts of destiny and the feelings of fear that come with night.[6]

We can picture the funeral hearse and the boy's experience of it like Kokoschka's early work, those paintings in which color has little significance and the lighter areas, encircled by darkness, conceal a melancholy light.

In this instance, the life-transition took the form of a profound pictorial impression, characteristic for the destiny of a painter. But the content of the picture— death—remained a motif in Kokoschka's life and took precedence again and again in his work.

***

For the musical conductor Bruno Walter (1876-1962) it was an auditory impression that was important. In fact, visual impressions had to disappear, dissolve, and die away. He was "listening" to the experience of transition.

Even when I was growing up, when I was a boy, I was often in a strange state of "dreaming"—an absorption into nothing in particular, a being out of myself— during which all the wheels usually turned by the rushing stream of outer or inner experience with such vehemence came to a halt, as though turned off, and stood still. I still remember how I first felt such a stillness as a melancholy emotion, weighing my spirits down. I still feel what I felt then, and can still see the place before me where, at the age of ten or eleven, I experienced this inner quivering. How it happened that I was standing alone in the school playground I can no longer remember; perhaps I had been kept late after school. I came into the big playground, which until then I had only known as filled with the noise of boys milling around and playing and which accordingly now seemed twice as empty and forsaken. I see myself standing there, overwhelmed by the deep stillness, and as I listened to it and to the slight wind that was blowing, I felt how out of the loneliness something unknown and mighty was taking hold of my heart. It was the first intimation to me that I was an ego, my first dawning feeling that I had a soul and that from somewhere or other it was being called upon.[7]

***

The Italian poet, Dante Alighieri (1265-1321) was only a boy of nine years when he met a girl about his own age in a street in Florence. She had probably grown up in the same neighborhood. This girl was named Beatrice; her name means "She who blesses." Their merely fleeting encounter as they passed each other had the deepest possible effect on the boy. As if in a condition that reaches beyond ordinary consciousness, he became aware of inner voices that spoke to him. As a poet, Dante later gave expression to this experience in his book *Vita Nuova*:

> For the ninth time since my birth, the light of heaven had already returned to nearly the same point in its rotation when the radiant mistress of my spirit appeared, who by many of those who did not know what to call her was called Beatrice. At that time, she had already been here in this life for as long as it takes the starry heavens to move eastward the twelfth part of a degree, so that she appeared before me at about the beginning of her ninth year, and I beheld her about the

end of my own ninth year. She appeared to me in a garment of noblest hue, crimson, modest and honorable, girded and adorned in a way befitting her very young age. At that moment, as I can truly say, the spirit of life, which dwells in the most secret chamber of the heart, began to tremble so violently that in the lightest pulses of my blood it seemed awesome to me, and, trembling, it spoke these words: "Behold, a god who is stronger than I and who comes hither and will rule over me." At this moment, the animal spirit, which dwells in that lofty chamber where all the spirits of our senses bring their perceptions, began to wonder greatly, and speaking in particular to the spirits of seeing, said these words: "Now your blessedness has revealed itself." Now the natural spirit, which inhabits that part where our nourishing takes place, began to weep, and said amid its tears: "Woe is me, poor fellow, for now I shall often meet with hindrance."

Although the children lived in the same neighborhood, it was not until nine years later that Dante met Beatrice again. He was twenty-seven when he wrote the following account of it:

Clad all in white, between two noble ladies, she turned her eyes to where I was standing in great trepidation; and in her inexpressible graciousness, which has now found its reward in a higher world, she greeted me so virtuously that I thought myself to behold then and there the farthest limits of blessedness.

There was no question of a union between the two, for already as a child Dante had been betrothed to Gemma Donati, and when Beatrice was twenty, she married the wealthy Simone dei Bardi. She died four years later.

Even more than when she was alive, Dante felt inspired by Beatrice after her death. He resolved to say of her "what no one had ever before said about a mortal being." In his chief work, *The Divine Comedy*, it is the figure of Beatrice who leads the poet in Paradise into the highest realms of inner vision accessible to her.

The people of Florence have paid homage to Dante and to Beatrice by placing statues of them both on the Ponte Vecchio. Dante and Beatrice greet each other across the roadway of the bridge.

What turned out to be the greatest event in the life of the poet began with a ninth year experience. *Incipit Vita Nuova*, or "Here Begins the New Life," is the title Dante placed at the head of his narrative.

***

In the autobiography of Rudolf Steiner (1861-1925) we find the following words:

> Toward Wiener-Neustadt and still further away toward the Steiermark, the mountains descend to the plain. The River Laytha winds its way through this plain. On the mountainside, there was a Redemptorine monastery. I often met the monks on my walks. I still recall how much I would have liked for them to speak to me, but they never did. As a consequence, these encounters made an undefined, though solemn impression on me that followed me long afterwards. It was in my ninth year that the idea firmly took root in me: The tasks of these monks must be connected with important things, and I must find out about them. Here again was a situation where I was full of questions that I had to carry around in me without getting answers. Yes, these questions about all kinds of things made me very lonely in my boyhood.

47

Rudolf Steiner goes on to describe how he first came to know what happiness was after this experience of loneliness.

Soon after my entry into the school in Neudörfl, I discovered in the assistant teacher's room a book on geometry. I was on such good terms with this teacher that without further ado I was allowed to borrow the book for my own studies. I went at it with enthusiasm, and for weeks my soul was filled with congruence, the similarity of triangles, quadrangles, and polygons. I pondered much on the question where parallel lines really intersect, and was enchanted by the theorem of Pythagoras.

The fact that the soul could live in constructing forms that were only inwardly perceived, without recourse to sense-impressions from the outside, gave me the greatest satisfaction . . . I know that it was through geometry that I first learned what happiness was.

I have to describe my relationship to geometry as the first budding of a view that gradually developed in me. It was already living more or less unconsciously in me during my earlier childhood but assumed a definite, fully conscious form around my twentieth year. I said to myself: the objects and processes perceived by the senses are in space; but just as there is this space outside man, so there is within him a kind of soul-space that is the scene for the activity of spiritual beings and processes. I could not regard thoughts merely as pictures we make of things, but I had to see them as revelations of a spiritual world in this soul-space. Geometry was for me a seemingly man-made knowledge that nevertheless had significance quite independent of human beings. Of course, I did not say this clearly to myself as a child, but I felt that one must be carrying the knowledge of the spiritual world in oneself as one does geometry.

For I was as sure of the reality of the spiritual world as I was of that of the sense-world. However, I needed some kind of justification for this; I wanted to be able to say to myself that the experience of the spiritual world is just as little an illusion as that of the sense-world. In geometry, I found, one *dares* to know something that only the soul experiences through its own activity. This feeling gave me the justification to speak of the spiritual world that I experienced just as I did of the sensory world. And I did speak of it in this way. I had two ideas that were certainly undefined, but that played a big part in my soul-life even before my eighth year: I distinguished between beings and things you can see and those you can't see.[8]

Thus, geometry became the bridge for the nine-year-old boy that could bring together two different worlds. Here we see Rudolf Steiner's life-motif shining forth. In his later years, standing firmly on the ground of the natural sciences of his day, Rudolf Steiner completed the building of the bridge between the sensory world and the spiritual, something no one had managed to do before him. In his work, this life-motif is visible everywhere.

***

"My first love was for words. As far back as I can remember, I was accompanied in my early days by solemnly spoken prayers and verses from the Bible. I felt them to be as much a vital necessity as the daily bread itself." In these words we can hear the primal theme of the life of a man who worked, in quite a special way, out of the creative forces contained in language. As educator and composer of verses for the report cards of his pupils, Heinz Müller (1899-1968), a Waldorf teacher, was able to unite the powers of language, the force of the Logos, with education.

His book *Healing Forces in the Word and its Rhythms,* published a year before he died, throws light upon his work.[9] Wolfgang Schad found the following beautiful words for the new edition of this book: "The healing power of language and the use of it in pedagogy were motives for Heinz Müller that have imprinted themselves into his biography." What form then did the transition in the ninth year take for this man?

In his autobiography, we see what the future teacher experienced—significantly enough in a classroom—at this important moment of his life.

When I was about ten years old, I had to take the entrance exam for the classical secondary school, the *Gymnasium.* As I was exempted from the oral test in arithmetic, I was finished with the exam before the other students and was taken into a senior class; there I experienced the first history lesson of my life. I had never before heard of the events the teacher spoke about; yet they seemed somehow familiar to me out of a long-distant past. Pictures arose in me on which my imagination worked in the liveliest fashion. What I heard did not always harmonize with what I was inwardly seeing. I have often since wondered about such a strange experience as this; I had certainly never before heard anything about the conflagration in Ephesus or the birth of Alexander the Great during the night of that catastrophe, and yet I seemed to be closely familiar with many scenes of these events. Vividly, the teacher described the event that destroyed one of the seven wonders of the ancient world. Moreover, there came from the teacher's lips, words that were full of mysterious meaning to me, such as "mystery-wisdom" and "self-knowledge," and Greek words that had once been heard in Diana's temple and that were to resound again at the beginning of the Gospel of John.

Although I listened to all this with great intensity, I saw a great deal in my mind that deviated from the teacher's account. In the events that arose before my youthful soul, there stood out particularly clearly the burning temple, mirrored in the waters of a bay, and the flame-illuminated marble steps that led up to it from the shore. (In 1910, it was not yet known that the temple of Ephesus had in fact stood at the edge of a sea inlet that had silted up later on.)

For days after this experience, something like a question lived in me: How did I come up with just these pictures, which arose in my soul as clearly as memories? My first history lesson was so full of questions and mysteries to me that everything else I experienced at that time paled beside it. After my first reading of the first verses of the Gospel of John, I was naturally none the wiser, but indeed even more perplexed and unsettled. Later, when I heard these same words for the first time in Greek, spoken by an older student, the sounds made a very deep impression on me, but of course answered none of the questions I found so puzzling. I tried to put them aside, but every attempt at evasion was futile. Something far too powerful had been stirred up in my soul through this first history lesson.[10]

What was it that lived above all else in the Ephesian Mysteries of Artemis? Rudolf Steiner described that the primeval creative Word was taught there and that this Word contained what leads to the beginning of the Gospel of John.[11] And it was precisely the opening words of this Gospel that Heinz Müller met through destiny when he was a student-teacher at the Waldorf School in Stuttgart. He describes the occasion as follows:

Eleven years later, I encountered the first words of the Gospel of John again in a special moment of destiny.

51

On the previous day, I had received permission to visit classes as student-teacher the next morning at the Waldorf School in Stuttgart. I went there quite early and walked up and down in front of the school, watching the teachers and children as they came from all directions. And now, ascending the last steps with a heavy tread, a man with a big head and rustic, strongly marked features came into view. He stopped in astonishment when I said hello to him. He looked at me inquiringly, and then said, "We haven't met before, have we?" When I said we had not, he continued, "Now isn't that a real pleasure? A lovely morning like this, with sunshine and birds chirping away, and here there is a young man standing before me whom I don't know, and he greets me like a friend." He said other things too with an intonation unmistakably Austrian, and then came suddenly an unexpected turn: "My name is Karl; what is yours?" "Heinz," I said. "Heinz, we are good friends. Come along with me; I have to go over to the Waldorf School to my children." Thus, it was that I entered the grounds of the school at the side of Dr. Karl Schubert. While he went into a wooden building to his class, I went to the school office and asked Rudolf Steiner what class I was to visit. He told me how to get to a certain classroom; I was to knock on the door and say that I had been sent by him to observe. I knocked and shortly thereafter Schubert opened the door. "I thought you would be coming to me today," he said and at once introduced me to his class. There were children of all ages, some to get special help for a few weeks or months before returning to their regular grade, and others who needed help all the time. I was a lot taller than Schubert, and he stood behind me with his hands on my shoulders, peeping around me, first on one side and then the other. Then he said, "Dear children, I am very happy today, for a good friend has come to visit us. And as I like him so much, you must like him as well." I then tried to go and sit unobtrusively at the back of the room but Schubert would not have that at all; instead, he gave me something special to do. He called out a big and clumsy lad, who had to be encouraged to speak, as Schubert put it. He had been repeating the first words of the Gospel of John with him every day, and I was now to take over this task. With each word in Greek, which had to be spoken out loud, the boy had to stamp his foot. So after the morning verse and some exercises that all the children did together, I took charge of the boy and set about speaking and stamping.

Meanwhile it had become very hot in the room; the sun was shining directly into the open windows. It sent its heat through the flat roof of the wooden building, which was covered with black roofing felt.

Karl Schubert taught the rest of the class while the boy and I stamped and declaimed our Ἐν ἀρχῇ... behind him. Suddenly he turned round and asked why I was saying it so quietly. Couldn't I do it louder? I said I would then disturb his own teaching. He would not accept this, and in a stentorian voice demonstrated how he wanted it done. Then there began for us a strenuous sweat cure, for the longer it went on the more energetically I had to urge on the awkward young man beside me to do his stamping. Finally, after about fifty minutes of this, the two of us came to an exhausted halt for a breather at the open window. Then in something between a sigh and a groan, but unmistakably approximating the words we had just been practicing, there came forth from the mouth of the panting youth Ἐν ἀρχῇ ἦν ὁ λόγος. For each word he used a deep, full breath. Turning round, Karl Schubert listened with the closest attention, and clapped first the boy and then me on the shoulder, proclaiming jubilantly, "I knew it right from the start this morning. It is a glorious day, the sun is shining, the birds are singing, a young friend greets me—and you, my boy, have spoken the first words in your life."[12]

53

A further destiny connection with speech was due to a bodily factor. Heinz Müller quickly became hoarse when teaching. After teaching only two lessons, he was unable to speak aloud. And because of this hoarseness he approached Rudolf Steiner: "You gave the colleagues at the Waldorf School a great deal in the way of speech exercises during the preparatory course before the school began. Would it be possible for you one day to give advice on what to do to correct one's own mistakes and deficiencies in speaking, and to work in a healing and pedagogical way through speech?"[13]

Rudolf Steiner then invited Müller to a course in speech formation in Dornach, which evidently resulted in the elimination of the hoarseness, for Müller never mentioned this problem again. In addition, Heinz Müller had important conversations with Rudolf Steiner about the way in which the healing-force in speech could flow directly into the teaching. He writes of this Dornach course as follows:

> Nearly everything that Rudolf Steiner then worked out for the first time in a small circle appeared two years later in the Drama Course, and can be studied in detail there. The second part of the question I had initially asked was dealt with in many conversations during the course of those two years; for the most part they consisted of brief suggestions and observations that Rudolf Steiner made whenever I told him of the difficulties of particular pupils of mine.
>
> One of the first things he said was: "Cultivate speech in yourself and your children with the greatest care, since far and away most of what a teacher gives his pupils comes to them on the wings of speech." When talking to children, one should never use a banal expression out of mere carelessness. Which of course does not mean one should go in for high-flown language. "Banality and empty pathos shut out real

heart and especially real humor straight away. These two, however, are a teacher's most important helpers as he shepherds his flock along."[14]

If we know Heinz Müller's biography and look back on the vision the boy had when he was about ten—the burning temple of Ephesus—we can sense the inner connection between the ancient Mystery center and the teacher's efforts to bring the healing power of speech to his children. This is the motif of his destiny that suddenly blazed forth between his ninth and tenth year. Past and future become visible as if in a moment of illuminated consciousness—only to sink down again out of sight. One is moved to astonishment and still more to reverence by the fact that it was Heinz Müller who stood next to Rudolf Steiner when the fire at the Goetheanum broke out and who, at Steiner's command, had to smash a hole in the wall so that the source of the fire could be seen. The building now in flames had itself been a house of the Word.

Three years after the Goetheanum had fallen victim to the flames, Heinz Müller began to teach in the Free Goethe School in Hamburg-Wandsbek. For forty-two years, he devoted himself wholeheartedly to Waldorf pedagogy and was able to let the power of the Logos flow into it more abundantly than almost anyone else before or since.

Thus, education received a new creative impulse. "Through the supersensible within the sensible, with the rediscovery of the Spirit, which had been lost from the Word, from the Logos, when the latter became an idol— with this rediscovery of the Spirit, there began a new era in education."[15]

Part Two

Understanding the Human Being
on the Basis
of the Ninth Year Experience

The Second Seven Years

A particular age in life, such as the ninth year, can best be studied if we survey the larger period in which it occurs. In this case we turn to the years that extend from school entry to about the age of fourteen or fifteen. This period comprises the second seven year phase of childhood, which manifests in both the inner development of soul and spirit and the growth of the body and may be subdivided into three periods.[1]

If we consider first of all the shaping forces working in the body, we can see a first phase beginning in the head with the change of the teeth. Then with the transition from the ninth to the tenth year follows the elaboration of the rhythmic system of heart and lungs, and this in turn is succeeded by the "awkward age," the adolescent years between twelve and fourteen when the limbs and the body's metabolism are further developed and the sexual organs come to maturity. In these three phases, the growth-forces of the body successively shape the form of head, trunk, and limbs.

The soul-spiritual development of the child keeps pace with the growth of the body. When the children first enter school, their imitative powers still predominate though the change of teeth has already begun. As more and more of the children's permanent teeth push through their gums, the imitative capacity dwindles away. When children have produced twice as many second teeth as they have baby teeth left, we can say that they have reached teeth-maturity, and they now have very little left of their imitative capacities. This is the situation at the entry into the transition at the age of nine. In the second developmental phase, the growth-processes move from the head to the heart and lungs. It is now that maturity in breathing is attained and the child enters the "factual age." This is the balanced middle period of childhood. In the third phase, when the growth-processes move into metabolism and limbs, "earth-maturity" is beginning; the factual age comes to an end, and the awkward age begins. Thus, the growth process reaches three successive peaks: teeth-maturity, breathing-maturity and earth- maturity, which correspond to the three phases of inner development: imitation, factual age, and adolescence.

In this step-by-step development during the second seven-year phase, particular areas of the body are alternately taking the lead; however, this gradual development occurs always in harmony with the whole. Thus, during the change of teeth, when the head development predominates, the forces of will are of course also active in the metabolic-limb region and depend on a regular rhythm in the children's daily life. In the second phase, the polar forces of head and will support the forming of the rhythmic system and help it reach its full growth and maturity in the area of heart and lungs. In the third phase, the head and the rhythmic system work in harmony upon the metabolic-limb system, thus bringing about the development of earth-maturity. Diagram 1 illustrates these processes.

This diagram is based on the sketch of the threefold human being that Rudolf Steiner used in various education courses. The successive stages in bodily development are indicated by the darker shading of head, trunk, and limbs. This bodily development is paralleled in the sphere of soul and spirit, by the phases of imitation, factual age, and adolescent years. The arrows indicate how at each step two

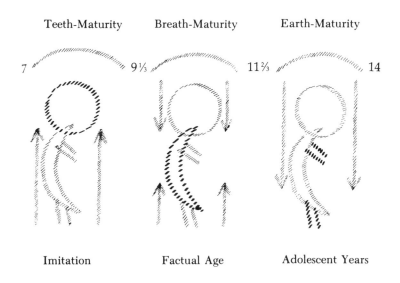

Teeth-Maturity	Breath-Maturity	Earth-Maturity

7   9⅓   11⅔   14

Imitation	Factual Age	Adolescent Years

Diagram 1. The Three Developmental Phases of the Child

systems bring their forces to bear on the remaining third one that is undergoing major development.

Thus, between the ages of seven and fourteen, there are two decisive transitions, one at nine and the other at twelve. As we are only concerned with the change at nine, let us compare the seven-year-old child with the twelve-year-old. In this way, we can define the period in which this transition takes place.[2]

61

Children at Seven and Twelve: A Comparison

The Limbs

The difference between first and six graders as far as their limbs are concerned is striking. The movements of the younger children are all lightness and grace as they chase each other around the teacher. The older children are much heavier in their movements; they move with a certain weariness. Their movements are often spasmodic; they seem to alternate erratically between standing still and suddenly making off at a run. They frequently lose their balance, stumble and even fall; lanky-legged, they walk about as if in a dream.

And how different is the handshake of the younger children compared to that of the older children! Before school in the morning, the little ones rush in to greet the teacher; a crowd of hands, warm and friendly reach out together. Some children even return to the end of the line to shake the teacher's hand again. In contrast, the sixth graders often have to overcome a slight reluctance to reach out their hand, which often as not is damp and cold. In the first grade, the teacher could do with thirty hands; in the sixth, two sometimes seem more than enough.

Another difference is in the length of the children's limbs relative to the rest of their bodies. Younger children, reaching over their head with their right arm, can just barely touch the tip of their left ear with their fingers, whereas sixth grade pupils can often cover the whole of their ear with their hand. Comparing seven-year-olds and twelve-year-olds, we see the contrast between the relatively shortest and relatively longest limbs during childhood. This in turn is an indication that the younger and older children have a completely different relationship to their limbs. The short limbs of the seven-year-olds are awake, active, and in joyful movement. It is through them that the children connect themselves with their surroundings. It is their hands and even feet that want to learn and not so much the head. Little hands roll a lump of modelling wax into a long sausage and then wind it up into a snail's house. In doing this, the children have in fact literally "grasped" the nature of the spiral. Stepping, hopping, and clapping, the children recite the various multiplication tables, and by way of their limbs learn them with very little effort.

The limbs of the older children are proportionately longer in relation to the rest of the body and are often heavy and weary and easily fatigued. At this age, the activity of the limbs not only serves to awaken the youngsters or help them memorize, but also does the reverse, namely, carry out an idea. For example, when an older child is carving a wooden bowl, he already has the idea of the finished bowl in mind, to some extent at least. The hands change the shape of the piece of wood until it has taken on the bowl-form imagined for it. The object is changed, awakened, so to say, into form through the limbs, whereas the seven-year-old is still giving form to himself. Through the activity of his limbs, he gradually comes to a certain understanding; he awakens when he does something with his hands or feet.

Up to a point we are justified in objecting here that older children also work on themselves through what they do and that the younger children, for instance, when shaping the wax have also changed the form of an object, namely the wax, besides understanding the spiral. However, we must not overlook that the seven-year-olds become aware of the form, the spiral, only at the end of their activity, while the older children have something of a consciousness of form to begin with, and this they then impose on the object, in this case, the wood. The processes run in entirely opposite directions:

First Graders: form themselves through the activity of their limbs (becoming conscious).

Sixth Graders: form the object through the activity of their limbs (giving form, creating).

This comparison of first and sixth graders shows that the forces working on the head and those working on the limbs have been inverted. In this reversal, the ninth year, as we shall see later on, is a highly significant turning point.

Having examined the contrast in the limbs, we must now look more closely at the transformation that takes place in the head.

The Head

The little faces of the children starting first grade are round and soft. Their round cheeks, their stubby little noses, and especially their teeth are still being formed. Their starry eyes, even with all their mirth, still have something dreamy about them. The fluctuating sense-impressions seem to penetrate into the children from outside as if to work on their still sleeping head and give it a more finely developed form.

In contrast to this, the twelve-year-olds present us with features that are already defined; their lips are full or thin, their noses are perhaps quite pronounced, and their eyes are far more awake. The childhood face has developed into a more personal countenance with an alert look. The whole face is now more clearly formed and defined, and the change of teeth is usually over by this time.

As has been said already, the younger children have relatively larger heads; in contrast, the older children have smaller heads relative to the rest of their body. Concerning large- and small-headed children, Rudolf Steiner pointed out that the former are rich in fantasy while the latter have little imagination but a better memory. This can also be applied to the two different ages.

While the formative forces of the organism are working on the form of the younger children's heads—as can be clearly seen in the change of teeth—the spiritual forces of the head are still asleep. At a young age, outer impressions are accepted only in a half-waking condition, that is, they are formed into colorful flowing pictures that are not as precisely formed as thoughts. Young children enjoy listening to their teacher tell a fairy tale, at times cradling their head in their little arms and completely absorbed into their own picture-world.

When the teacher is telling of "Little Red Riding Hood," of the woodland flowers she gathers for her grandmother, and of the wolf, he uses elements from the ordinary world but deals with them imaginatively. The red hood indicates the girl's sanguine nature, the flowers represent the charm and attraction of the sense-world, and the wolf symbolizes the forces within the body's metabolic-limb system that overpower the intellectual forces of the head. The children experience the wolf the same way an adult would experience a net of evil intentions closing in around him.

Fairy tales communicate something true and full of wisdom to the imagination; however, on the level of thoughts and ideas they appear enigmatic or even merely fantastic. It is by way of the imagination that fairy tales lead children to the realities of waking life. They are similar to the dreams we sometimes have right before waking up; in them, too, the nature of certain objects around us is revealed more clearly.

Let us now look at what goes on in the heads of twelve-year-olds. Here, we shall see that in the two ages the processes run in opposite directions, just as they do in the limb area. By the age of twelve, students are ready for their first lessons in physics.[1] We can begin these with a simple experiment. We show how light changes while passing through a glass filled with water that has been darkened gradually with an appropriate solution. If we are to observe accurately, we must stand back a little. In psychological terms, this is a position or attitude of antipathy. The object under observation is to be seen just as it is, without being in any way altered or affected by the observer himself.

The students see the light from the electric bulb change from yellow to orange and finally to red; they will see that the water, in becoming opaque, appears blue. How different is the experience of the first graders as they listen in warmest sympathy to the story-telling of the teacher! On the following day, the students must recall the experiment; the object of observation is no longer experienced in the outer world, but is only remembered. Now a heightened detachment, a more intense "antipathy" is necessary to ensure that no distortions out of the student's own soul affect the recollection. Again, we find things are very different with the seven-year-olds: their memory is warmed by the sympathy with which they listen to the voice of the teacher and by the play of their fantasy.

On the third day, the sixth graders must think about the color experiment. They grasp something of the laws of color when they come to see that it is the nature of light to become active when passing through an opaque medium; as a result the colors yellow, orange, and red appear. The passive quality of darkness reveals itself to the children in the blue opaque water, illuminated by the light. Thus, students attain quite an individual relationship to the process through which colors come into being. In a way, the inner perceptions of the seven- and twelve-year-olds meet at this point. And yet what a difference! The first grader listening devoutly and full of playful fantasy to the voice of the teacher takes in the flow of pictures as though from a spring welling up within his own being. Similarly, the older children experience within themselves the wellspring of light that has flown out and has manifested itself in colors.

The younger children immerse themselves easily into this imaginative world; it readily opens up for them when they can quietly listen to the teacher's voice. The older students, on the other hand, need several days for an external impression to deepen enough within them before they can grasp it imaginatively.

Thus we can summarize the processes in the head region of the seven-year-old child and the twelve-year-old one as follows:

First Grader: The still sleeping spirit in the head weaves in the imaginative realm and then awakens to the right understanding for the sensory world.

Sixth Grader: The spirit in the head, now fully awake, penetrates into the sensory world and discovers the imaginative realm in the sleeping depths of its own soul.

The Trunk

Having found a distinct contrast in the development of the systems of limbs and head, we must now see if there is also such a difference in the trunk organization. In the first place, it is a striking fact that when first graders sit next to sixth graders, the difference in height is not nearly as great as it is when they stand next to each other. Sittingheights and standing-heights are noticeably different. Again, at the younger age, the trunk has something of a cylindrical shape, with the comfortably rounded tummy of small children. In the sixth grade, however, particularly the girls' waists are already well-defined and, as often as not, are girdled to produce a "wasp-waist." During this pre-puberty phase, children also often tend to put on more weight. In sixth grade boys, the body takes on a more differentiated form; the bone structure becomes more apparent, in strong contrast to the softness predominating in younger boys and girls alike.

The rhythmic system centered in the chest in heart and lungs is expressed in the soul in the emotional life. In the younger children, the breathing dominates here, that is, they breathe lightly and quickly, without completely filling the lungs. In the older children, especially the boys, the movement of the rib cage in breathing indicates a more complete aeration. Their breathing is deeper and relatively slower.

There is a difference between the two ages in the tempo of the pulse-beat; for all their quicker breathing, younger children have a relatively slower pulse.[2] This predominance of the breath in the pulse-breath ratio is paralleled in the soul development: impressions from their surroundings— to which, after all, the air they breathe connects them—can easily overwhelm younger children, who are often unable to fend them off. Even when tears are still trickling down their cheeks due to some outer event, the younger children can already start laughing again because of another outer happening. Nothing shows more clearly the extent to which the feelings of little children are determined by the world around them.

Twelve-year-olds have slower breathing, but a relatively quicker pulse. They can be beset from within by strong emotions, borne upwards on the waves of the blood from the sphere of the metabolism, just as seven-year-olds can easily be overwhelmed by their surroundings.

Thus, we see that the first graders are completely interwoven with the world around them through a basic mood of sympathy; in essence, they do not oppose any feelings of their own to the world surrounding them. However, the twelve-year-olds, due to the feelings rising up out of their own organism and as yet not related to the outer world, can develop a resistant attitude towards the world. Such antipathy, though at first bound to the body, is essential if exact ideas of the outer world are to be formed. The science classes beginning in sixth grade appropriately support this antipathy.

The contrasting ways of experiencing in the two ages is illustrated by the following two examples:

1. Example of antipathy bound to the body:

During the break between lessons, the children in the sixth grade have gone out into the playground. One girl, however, has stayed behind at her desk, her head resting on her clenched fists and her eyes closed. For no visible outer reason she is in emotional turmoil to the point that one might think her heart was near bursting. At last she sighs, beats two or three times on the desk with her fists, rises and walks to the door. The teacher asks sympathetically, "What is the matter?" "Nothing," the student says reassuringly and calmly. "Really, nothing at all," and with a laugh she goes out to join the others.

Such an occurrence hardly happens with younger children but is quite common with children entering puberty. The forces of antipathy rise up out of the body, and the child withdraws completely from his or her surroundings, though perhaps only for a little while. At this age, it is not the outer world but the one within, shaped by so many disturbing influences rising up out of the body, that chiefly determines the child's emotional life. Generally speaking, children at this age are not able to say why they feel as they do. Similarly, seven-year-olds are not aware of what is prompting a particular response on their part; they are largely influenced by the outside through their capacity for imitation, which works on their body.

2. Example of the outside influencing the child through sympathy:

A girl in the first grade has uttered some nasty, ugly words. Disappointed, the teacher says to the class, "You probably did not hear it, but one of you has just said something very ugly."

"I know," some children near her call out in unison. A boy among them, wanting to repeat the words, eagerly raises his hand. The teacher asks him to repeat those ugly words because she herself finds it impossible to say such words. The boy stands up, but on looking at the sad face of the teacher, he is also inwardly affected, and says in a whisper, "I can't say them either."

Summary:

Our essential findings can be listed in the following table:

	First Grader	Sixth Grader
Head	Big	Small
	Imaginative	Abstractly thinking
	Asleep	Awake
Trunk	Rounded	Slender, small
	Life interwoven with	Inner life
	the surrounding world	
	Asleep	Dreaming
Limbs	Short	Long
	Related to	Related to
	surroundings	the inner life
	Awake	Asleep

The differences in head, trunk, and limbs we have seen between six-year-olds and twelve-year-olds can, of course, also be found in a comparison between five-year-olds and fourteen-year-olds. The greater the distance on either side from the turning point at the age of nine, the more distinct are the contrasts.

The Child in the Ninth Year Transition

The Move Within One's Own House

The comparison of seven- and twelve-year-old children shows that a profound change has taken place both inwardly and outwardly between these ages. All three systems of the threefold human being have been metamorphosed. One could say that the children have "moved within their own house," have taken more completely possession of their own house. The question now arises whether there is a certain regularity or law underlying this event.

Rudolf Steiner once spoke of a stream that seeped away in one place and then welled up again somewhere else; he compared certain soul-processes in human beings with this phenomenon in nature. Such processes can vanish into the inner depths of the human being, to emerge again at a later time in a changed form. If we consider the differences between children at the ages of seven and twelve from this point of view, we find, for instance, that certain characteristics of the head region in seven-year-olds disappear and show themselves again in the limb system of twelve-year-olds. Younger children have large heads relative to the rest of their body; they live sleepily in their own fantasy world, just as the long legs of older children, as we have indicated above, are "sleepy" and are associated with their own inner world. Similarly, the limbs of seven-year-olds are short, and livingly connected with the surroundings, and they are awake. These characteristics also vanish and reappear later on in the head of older children. The head of a twelve-year-old is relatively small; the child develops an active relationship to the world through the activity of nerves and senses, and the spiritual forces of the head are awake. We have also found this rearrangement of characteristics in the rhythmic system. The older children no longer merely imitate their environment, but come to have inner experiences of their own, which they can consciously set against their surroundings.

How does this exchange come about? Doesn't this presuppose a kind of inner "remodeling" in which both the forces from above and from below play a part? This assumption is confirmed by the phenomena that can be seen in the rhythmical processes of blood circulation and breathing. The movement from above down is expressed in breathing in the stronger and deeper activity of the lungs. This transition—resembling a descending rhythm—is countered from below by another movement. This ascending rhythm comes up out of the blood, out of the metabolism, and surges up the stronger the closer the child gets to puberty.[1]

Both pulse and breathing are an expression of the harmony in a human being who is at one with himself. They are in balance when four pulse-beats accompany one breath of in- and out-breathing. Hadumoth Rötges, a school doctor, indicates how the "ascending pulse-curve and the descending breath-curve meet each other" approximately at the ninth year, the two forces counterbalancing each other for a short time in the ratio of 1:4.[2] This means that neither the blood nor the breathing predominate; they are in harmony with one another. In this moment of transition, "the ego links itself to the metabolism," and the children experience themselves as separate from the world, as standing over against it, as egos.[3]

74

Thus, the children's "move within their own house" is stimulated by the rhythmic system by way of breathing and blood circulation. This "move" can best be mapped out by a diagram clarifying the ascending and descending movements.

The schematic representation of the threefold human being that Rudolf Steiner used is particularly helpful here.[4] The geometrical figures on which the drawing is based— line, moon crescent, and circle—can be made to metamorphose into each other through movement. Through continuing swelling in one direction, the circle first turns into a crescent and ultimately opens up into the line; by contracting again it returns to itself—the curve in the middle section being formed first from the outside and then from the inside. Brought into movement, the figure thus presents the metamorphoses from limbs through trunk to head and from head through trunk to limbs, a process that cannot be observed on the physical level but only on the soul-spiritual one.

Two such forms facing each other, as in the diagram below, can represent the seven-year-old and the twelve-year-old child. With one line we can trace the ascending movement from the limb-sphere of the first grader to the head-sphere of the sixth grader, and another line can represent the descending movement from the head-sphere of the younger to the limb-sphere of the older child. The change in the rhythmic system is indicated by a circle. The seven-year-old's impressions, which the child mostly receives from his surroundings, are represented by arrows approaching from the outside, whereas the personal feelings, which the older pupil brings to the world, are represented by arrows opposing the ones coming from the outside.

First Grader   Sixth Grader

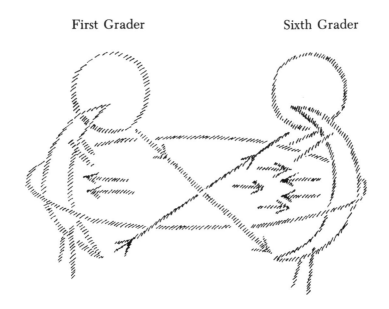

The "life-transition" in the ninth year, as Rudolf Steiner called it, lies exactly at the intersection of the lines representing this development. If we want to come to a better understanding of this crossing point or turning point, we have to inquire into the significance of the reversal of head-forces and limb-forces.

What would result for the growing human being if the spiritual forces of his head continued to sleep, his impressions full of fantasy, and his perceptions tied to the environment through imitation? It becomes at once obvious that in this case the environment would continue to determine the human being. There would be no possibility of either separating from the world, reflecting upon it, or engendering thought-impulses from within our own mind. The ego must be able to make its way into the functions of the head, for only then is it possible for us to form thoughts free from outer and inner influences.

Furthermore, we can ask what would happen to our limb-metabolic system if our limbs retained only the awake perceptive character they possess in little children. In this case, we would have to forego any kind of purposive transformation of our environment, for children hold back their creative forces within the sphere of their own fantasy, which they use up in playing. Thus, they have no power left to direct their activity upon an outer object in the way a sculptor, for instance, is able to do. The ego, therefore, must also be able to link itself to our will-impulses.

We find a similar situation in our middle system. If adults were to live solely in the feelings aroused by their surroundings, they would be helplessly exposed to the influences of sympathy and antipathy. They would lose that inner balance they can achieve precisely because they are able to experience themselves in the workings of antipathy and sympathy. They free themselves from the enchantment of the direct influence of sympathy and antipathy by raising them to the level of perception. This also is possible only through the ego, which develops within the feeling-sphere through perception.

Thus, we can see that in all three spheres of the soul the influence of the environment is predominant up to the ninth year. Then a whole epoch of life comes to an end with the drying up of the imitative capacity. A new impulse comes into play: the self as eternal individuality takes hold of the body through the transformation described above. The ego intervenes here in a transitional phase, that is, in a phase of unstable balance. The special difficulties of the ninth year transition are connected with this. In public schools they can be a significant factor when children fail the grade and have to repeat it, a problem that begins around this age.

The ninth year transition can be compared with a birth, for just as children physically free themselves from their mother's body at birth, so they now free their soul from the surroundings in which they have been living through imitation. And what is being born there needs similar protection and love from parents and educators.

How do children experience this transition? A trace of sadness is in their eyes; their gait is heavier than before, and they have become more sensitive. They become aware that their world, in which they felt so fully at home, has become strange to them. From time to time, they want to withdraw from it entirely. They are puzzled by the separation between themselves and the world; their father, mother, and their friends now stand outside the circle of their own world. They long to return; they long to be understood and to be loved. But something mysterious and puzzling stands in their way.

In this loneliness, the finest, most delicate feelings arise in children, and nothing must disturb this experience, neither pressure nor curiosity. It is in this loneliness that the child finds himself and becomes aware of his own ego. It is in his loneliness that the child senses that he will go out into life from the center of this ego.

It is tremendously important in what mood parents accompany their children through this difficult phase of life. Anxiety, the modern tendency to resignation, and the superficiality of life in big cities—all contribute to make this process more difficult. But if there is gladness of heart and if the children see how adults stand their ground in the face of the difficulties of their own destiny, then the spark of ego-affirmation grows. What happens during that time of transition can influence the rest of the child's life. As often as not, it is at this transition time that the development of the child into an ego-strong or an ego-weak personality is decided.[5]

How The Curriculum Helps

Everything Rudolf Steiner suggested in the curriculum for the third grade of the Waldorf School is meant to form a sheath for the reception of the child's I. For example, there are lessons in house building; walls are erected, a roof put over them, and the outer world is excluded. In this activity children experience the forming of their own inner space, and this experience of space is just what the children are seeking. In this way they find themselves. At this age, the children also learn about the work of the farmer. They plow the earth and sow the seed, and in the process they develop the following picture: "Just as the seed unfolds in the earth, so my I unfolds within my soul."

With the help of poetry in the language classes, which are especially emphasized in the Waldorf Schools, children gradually learn how they can, as it were, slip with their ego into the sounds of words and then conjure up pictures from these sounds, the seeds of language. When they achieve this, they experience how they can express themselves out of their own inner resources. The importance of story-telling at this time has been indicated in the chapter "Dear Parents."

In terms of music, children under the age of nine live chiefly in the pentatonic, a scale in which there is neither keynote nor half note. At the age of nine, they are led to the major and minor third. It is with delight that they experience the going out and coming in of major and minor keys as the movement of their own *I*.[6]

Since children reach breath-maturity during that year, the soprano recorder can now be used to support the development of breathing. Only when this phase of breath-development ends at about the twelfth year can wind instruments be chosen that require deeper and longer breaths, such as the transverse flute, the oboe, the clarinet, or the bassoon. Just as the recorder is the instrument of choice for the ninth year, so string instruments are preferred for the twelfth year because the children can now deepen their capacities on them in quite an essential way. The clumsiness of the limbs so characteristic for this age can be modified and overcome through the use of the bow. For these two critical passages at the ninth and twelfth years, music is an especially suitable therapy.

The help given by Rudolf Steiner's curriculum in the crisis of the ninth year is not confined to the lessons in the third grade. Instead, we can see that both curriculum and teaching method follow the principle of reversal through all grades from the first to the sixth. Physical development is paralleled by that of soul and spirit. To demonstrate this in detail is beyond the scope of this book, but the juxtaposition of the curriculum for the first and the sixth grades reveals this principle in broad outline.

Contrary to the generally prevailing practice of cramming the prescribed quota of knowledge into the still sleeping head of the first grader, in the Waldorf School it is not the head that learns at first, but the limbs: feet, arms, hands, fingers. Multiplication tables are recited to the accompaniment of hopping, jumping, stepping, clapping, or entertaining finger-play. It is the fingers that count, add, and subtract, and these fingers also learn to knit, and not only those on girls' hands. A special role is played by eurythmy, which allows the children to enter through movement into the great realm of speech-sounds. They can be a wave with *W*, a bear with *B*, a rolling wheel with *R*, or a water spring with the flowing *L*.

What becomes of these activities in the sixth grade? What develops out of all that the hands have perceived and understood? In the sixth grade, lessons in the natural sciences begin. The children now learn how to observe and how to think about their observations. Their thinking must be awake and vigorous if they are to grasp, conceptualize, and understand anything. What is now done in the realm of nerves and senses was previously carried out by the limbs: grasping and taking in.[7] What was before carried out by the limbs is now demanded of the nerves and senses.

Having traced the development from the awake limbs of the younger children to the awake head of the older children, we can now take the same course with the young pupils' dreaming head, for it is related to the "sleeping" limbs of the older pupils. The fairy tales we tell in first grade are full of wisdom, murmuring to the sleeping head-spirit of the little children like a dream before the moment of waking up. Inner pictures arise in the children; their fantasy is stimulated and becomes colorful, deep, and wide-ranging. As the children get older, the artistic impressions they have thus taken in appear to vanish as though into an inner abyss.

What becomes of them by the time the children enter their twelfth year? What the younger children have taken in dreamily and with seeming passivity then appears again in outer activity. It penetrates into the realm of the limbs, which are the organs of the will and allow us to influence and shape our environment.

The sixth graders can draw on the wellspring of artistic impressions that has been fed by the hearing and retelling of fairy tales. The inner picture-forms are now becoming a forming power, by virtue of which the twelve-year-olds give shape to all that they do with their hands. The curriculum provides them with many opportunities for such activity, for example, in various craft lessons and in gardening. In gymnastics and eurythmy the forming capacities of the limbs are called on in quite specific ways. These forces must be exerted lest the seed that was taken in by the sleeping spiritual forces of the head as though in a dream now rots away.

This change in development should be kept in mind when the frequent lament is heard that the creative powers of childhood have now run dry. When the heads of small children are fed only with intellectual content instead of the imaginative pictures of fairy tales, then they have indeed been robbed of their creative forces. In the same way, the children are prevented from becoming truly awake when they are forced from early on to keep their limbs still for long times, to sit still, such as on long car journeys.

In the middle sphere, too, we can see how the small children free themselves from the feelings that have bound them so closely to their surroundings; they become receptive to impressions that are not just subjective but also contribute to objective knowledge.

This can be best illustrated by an example given by Rudolf Steiner. In Torquay he told English teachers "The Story of the Violet" about a violet that came to fear that the vast blue sky above would one day deal it a dreadful blow, or so an ill-natured dog had said.[8] But the next day, a little lamb comforted the violet by saying, "The sky is so much bluer than you are in your tiny form, because it has so much more love than you can have in your smallness." Whereupon the little violet realized that it was under the protection of the great violet of the heavens.

How do the feelings the seven- or eight-year-old children had when they heard this simple story change when these same children think back to it at the age of twelve or thirteen? The older children grasp the connections in the story through thinking, and realize: "Look, this mighty sky-violet, this violet god, is entirely blue in its whole expanse. Now imagine a little bit cut out of it, and that is the little violet. In the same way, God is as great as the cosmic ocean. Your soul is a drop of God. But just as a drop of water out of the sea contains the same water as the sea, so your soul is the same as God, only just a tiny drop of it." In an especially beautiful way, this example shows that in teaching nothing cut and dried and no fixed, once-and-for-all definitions should be forced on the children. Instead, they must be taught in such a way that everything remains alive and thus able to grow with the children—even through the transition in the ninth year.

Disturbances in Thinking, Feeling, and Willing

Under current living conditions, there are not many children who go through the ninth year transition without some kind of physical indisposition. Children mostly complain of such symptoms as headaches or stomachaches, dizziness, heart palpitations, or difficulty in breathing. Rudolf Steiner mentioned these difficulties and stressed that if healthy child development is not possible, then "from these sicknesses all kinds of predispositions to illnesses will certainly remain behind for the entire rest of life." He further said: "Among the most obvious conditions that later accompany, say, anemia, are such symptoms as fatigue, limpness, difficulties in falling asleep and waking up." Pointing out that these symptoms appear to some extent in most children "any time between the change of teeth and puberty and reach their peak between the ninth and tenth years," Rudolf Steiner then suggested remedies physicians could use in treating these symptoms. "One has to take these things into account with most people, unless they have a robust 'peasant' constitution." If these difficulties manifesting in bodily symptoms in the head, in the rhythmic system and in the metabolism are not properly recognized and taken into account in pedagogy, then they can lead in later life to disturbances in thinking, feeling, and willing.[9]

The fairy tale "Snow White" shows us in a wonderful picture how the three systems of the human being are poisoned through the intellect that is personified by the wicked queen. With only a slight deviation, we could say: "Mirror, mirror on the wall, who is the fairest (that is, the top of the class) of them all?" It is the pressure to perform that constricts the breathing like the bodice laced too tightly, the report-card pressures that, like the poisoned comb in the hair, give rise to nervous troubles. Being kept behind to repeat a grade works like the poisoned apple and feeds the inferiority complex that can lame the will for the rest of life.

A pedagogy that takes the development of the child into account needs every support from the home. Every soulless impression, above all those coming from technology, does special damage during the ninth year transition. Are we always clear about the effects television, radio, tape recordings and long car rides have on children? Excessive concern about homework can harm not only the head but also the digestion, which is also affected by the transition in the ninth year. It is important that homework during this transitional period be reduced and that children be given food they can digest. It is a mistake to force children to eat at this time; it would be far more sensible to give smaller portions of easily digested food several times during the day. Disturbances in the rhythmic system, such as dizziness, palpitations, and shortness of breath, indicate that children during this period need an especially great deal of love to find the way into themselves. They will often come and ask for help because they cannot do this or that, but in reality they are asking for the "heartfelt, soul-warmed word."

The task of the adults is made more difficult at this time, for the children view their parents and teachers for the first time with sharply critical eyes, noticing every weakness with a newly awakened clear-sightedness. Accordingly, the educator must spare no effort to win a conscious relationship to those forces that lead us out of the narrow boundaries of our own personality.[10]

The Incarnation of the Ego

What impulses can be of special help to children in this difficult transition? How can they gain the forces for renewed development as unified beings? We will now point to three pictorial motifs that can nourish the religious experience of children, especially if we accompany them appropriately with our own thoughts and feelings. Through their separation from the world children experience their own ego-sphere. In this experience, however, there slumbers something still deeper, namely, the feeling of the immortality of their ego. The Biblical story of the creation confirms the children's inner sense that God created the human being. When they think of this divine origin, a divine element can light up in the earthly ego.

On the capital of a pillar in a Romanesque church, there is a representation of the theme of Genesis. God the Father breathes the living breath into Adam. The breath streaming forth from the mouth of God has the form of a plant-stem with leaves that make their way toward Adam. The blossom is already within Adam; the roots are still with God. Upside-down, the plant lowers itself into Adam. Pictures such as this of a plant growing inside the human being, having roots, leaves, and blossoms, come out of ancient traditions. They do not refer to the notion of a plant growing upright inside the human being just as it does outside, but to an image that grows from above down. This plant forms its hard roots in the bone structure of the head, where we are rooted in our thinking. The plant then unfolds its leaves, which allow it to breathe, in the region of the lungs, and its blossoms with stamens and pistil point downward.[1]

This notion of an upside-down plant can be understood in view of the reversal of life-forces in the ninth year. Though unable to understand this clearly, children nevertheless unconsciously experience that something is sinking into their life that is relevant to their whole individual existence.

It is not rare for children at this age to ask their parents if they really are their true father and mother. This question grows out of the children's strong experience of themselves as individual beings, having entered into earthly life not merely through the family or through heredity.[2] A completely different question is concealed behind the one the children ask, namely, the question of their own spiritual origin, and they seek the answer not in anything external, but in the realm of religion. How these thoughts can be brought in a pictorial way to children is illustrated in the appendix in the story "The Sturdy Sapling."

Another theme that provides children with good preparation for the ninth year transition is to be found in the legend of Christophorus. Ophorus, the giant, is determined to put his great strength at the service of the highest. First of all, he serves a mighty king. However, the king fears the devil, and so Ophorus then serves the devil himself. But the devil flees from the Cross. On the advice of a hermit, Ophorus now devotes himself to carrying travelers across a stream, in order to serve Christ through acts of neighborly love. Then one night, he is carrying a child whose enormous weight pushes him under water. It is the Christ-child, who thus baptizes him with the name Christ-Ophorus. Then, he must plant his staff in the earth.

This staff bears leaves and blossoms when Christophorus is found dead in his hut the next morning.

An extraordinary motif is presented in this legend. It points to a force of life, symbolized in the blossoming staff, that works on beyond the boundary of death. This image indicates that Christophorus has found the way to Christ through death. Such a legend—it is told to children in the second grade—can prepare the eight-year-old pupil for the coming transition in the ninth year.

In the ninth year, children meet with the eternal core of their being; they are now in a position to understand the mortality of mankind. This is often the first time that they consciously see a corpse. Thus, an awareness of both immortality and mortality can live in the children at the same time. However, they are not yet able to separate these two realms from each other. It is of immense importance for the whole of later life that they can experience through a narrative, such as that of Christopher, that even in death there lights up life.

A further life-motif can be understood if we consider the indication of Rudolf Steiner's that up to the ninth year art is a servant to children, but that after this time children should become a servant of art. This change results from the liberation of creative forces that had until then been active unconsciously in building up the body but that can now slowly and gradually be used to give expression to the ego. The creative core in the human being is now being addressed; through art it can reveal the spiritual in matter. For this reason, the artistic element is of central importance in Waldorf pedagogy.

Thus, there are three motifs that children in this age can take in: the divine origin of human beings, the lighting-up of life in death, and the realm of art. These three themes can become impulses that unite children—homeless as they have become during this crisis—with the world of the

Father, the Son, and the Holy Spirit. This whole process takes place in the sleeping regions of the children's soul. Later in life, these three impulses that were implanted around the ninth year can increasingly be taken up into consciousness.

A Word from the School Doctor

The turning point between the ninth and tenth year also manifests in bodily symptoms. At this age, the heart's capacity for blood intake—the so-called pulse-volume— suddenly increases by leaps and bounds. Thus, the organ that holds a central position among all the other organs increases its powers at the very moment when the central being of the child—the I or ego—undergoes a decisive turn in its development. That this transitional point represents something of a real crisis becomes clear through another bodily process, namely, in the behavior of the blood sugar.

The ego-experience has its physical foundation in the sugar content of the blood, which is influenced by the sugar in the diet. We all know that certain conditions of weakness that affect our feelings about ourselves can be overcome by eating a piece of sugar, a sweet fruit, or some other sweet food. (Of course, excessive sugar consumption can have unfavorable results.)

In the course of the childhood years, the sugar level steadily increases in proportion to the increasingly deeper incarnation of the child's ego. This ascending curve, however, shows a temporary descent exactly at the age of nine. There we have the physical counterpart to the tender I-experience that needs the support of the adults and appropriate educational measures. The weakness, loneliness, and feeling of abandonment that the nine-year-old child experiences is also expressed in the temporary sinking of the blood sugar level.

The symptoms of the so-called school-illness, which can occur at any time during the whole of the second seven year period, culminate around the ninth year. Children complain of pains in the head or the stomach, sickness, nausea, palpitations, shortness of breath (wheezing), dizziness, and weakness. Occasionally short-lived attacks of fever occur.

The mother complains that the child looks ill, is pale, and has shadows under his or her eyes. She reports the child's lack of appetite, nervousness, fatigue, and sleep disorders. The teacher notices that the child gets exhausted easily and is less able to concentrate. These symptoms are sometimes summarized as the "periodic syndrome" because they have a fluctuating character and alternate with each other. It never happens that all the symptoms are present at the same time. The same child who has first been suffering from a headache may be complaining some time later about stomach-aches. These symptoms often disappear very quickly. It may be that the doctor is called to a feverish child, whose trouble cannot be diagnosed at first. The next day, when the doctor arrives, the child is well again and in some cases may already be back in school.

Despite the elusive nature of the symptoms, they must be taken seriously. Abdominal symptoms may on occasion indicate appendicitis, especially since appendicitis finds its maximum occurrence during the second seven years. Other serious disorders, such as stomach ulcer or Crohn's disease, can be the underlying cause for abdominal pain. Therefore, one should not wait too long before consulting a physician about these symptoms.

In general, however, this second seven year period is the healthiest period during the whole of human life. The characteristic symptoms of school illness are almost always caused by external influences. They can emerge because of a disruption in the family situation (broken home), or because of an excessive amount of schoolwork (pressure to perform). Very often the cause lies in a massive overstimulation of the senses—above all on the way to school through traffic, shops, illuminated advertisements, and so forth—but also at home through television, cinema, and radio. In many cases, the children's diet is also a contributing factor, more often through too much rather than too little food. Meals should be eaten at regular intervals and not substituted by casual snacking between meals. Artificial additives and colorings should be avoided as much as possible.

There is no scientific explanation why children react in this way to external stresses—after all, we all have to cope with them in one way or another. Therefore, no specific treatment for school illness has been found. It is presumed, however, that all the symptoms associated with it, as varied as they are, have a common underlying cause. This cause lies in the unstable condition of the child that reaches a certain peak around this critical time in the ninth year.

During this period, children not only need the support of the adults around them and their educational measures, but also that of remedies. Rudolf Steiner recommended various modifications of iron for treating the symptoms of schoolchildren, for instance, iron carbonate for stomachaches, iron chloride for disorders of the heart and circulation, lemon iron for breathing difficulties, and finally pure iron as an effective remedy for school headaches. With such iron treatment, the physician actually follows nature herself, for in their natural development children receive each year a higher dose of iron in their blood. The iron level in the blood increases steadily until puberty. For the children born of "robust peasant blood," growing up in conditions just right for them—which actually even for such children can hardly be found anymore nowadays—nature herself provides all the iron treatment they need. In many cases, however, additional iron is necessary and has proven beneficial in the various forms of school illness. Under the guidance of iron the *I* works its way with certainty through the critical phase of the ninth year.

Dr. Walter Holtzapfel, M.D.

Part Three: Appendices

The Sturdy Sapling
The Half Moon-Nodes
The Reversal in the Change of Teeth
Rudolf Steiner's Indications for
Form Drawing

The Sturdy Sapling

Once upon a time there was a sunbeam that fell upon a rose-red blossom and there became a tiny seed. The wind carried this little seed high up into the sky; it flew over a deep chasm. In the chasm, it was dark, stony, and cold. Then the little seed became afraid that it might fall into the chasm, but the wind blew it farther and farther until it flew over a lake. The lake was blue, big, and deep; the little seed became afraid that it would fall into the lake, but the wind blew it farther and farther until it flew to where there was a great fire of burning straw, which the farmers had started. The seed began to whirl round and round in the smoke; it became hot and could no longer see anything. Once more it was afraid and thought it would surely perish now. At last the wind carried it down to a place in the woods, where it lay still and fell asleep.

When at last the seed awoke again, it had already grown into a beautiful young larch tree. It had firm roots, so that the wind could do nothing more to it; it spread out its branches toward the sun in order to gain strength. At last this tree came to bear tiny rose-red blossoms, so that the sunbeams came to it and it bore seeds. Then it remembered that it also had once been a sunbeam and then a seed, and that it had been very afraid over the deep chasm, over the big lake, and over the fire. Now, because it was so firmly rooted, it no longer had such fear. Now it was big and wise, and it dawned on the young tree that the earth was the body of God, the water the blood of God, the wind the breath of God, and that it had been sent down by God as a little sunbeam. And so it knew that everything that happened was by God's will. No hardship could come to it, unless God willed it so. Thus, the tree grew, became tall and strong, and no storm could trouble it.

The Half Moon-Nodes

The life-transition we have been considering is connected with great cosmic events: it is a reflection of forces we can see in the movements of sun and moon. Just as in the development of the child between the seventh and the twelfth year we see a reversal that begins in the ninth year, so after a period of nine and one-third years, so the moon reverses the relationship of its own orbit to that of the sun, the ecliptic. It now intersects the ecliptic at the same point (that is, the half moon-node) in an ascending arc where it had previously intersected in a descending direction. The astronomical reversal, as seen from the earth, may be represented as follows:

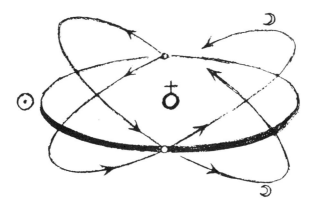

The ecliptic is intersected by the moon's orbit at the nodes in the direction of the arrows at an angle of 5°. The angle has been increased here for the sake of clarity.[1]

The moon's orbit intersects the solar ecliptic at the half moon-node in an ascending and then in a descending direction. After nine and one-third years, the moon's orbit has shifted so far that it moves through the same points in the opposite direction: where its orbit was descending before it is now ascending. The same happens at the nodal point on the opposite side of the ecliptic: the ascending moon-node crosses the descending one.

If education is to fulfill its task of leading the growth-processes in the children's soul-spirit nature ever farther, then the teacher must know and take into account the laws prevailing in the growth of the body. The archetypes of these laws can be discovered in the script of the stars, as we have here tried to show in the case of the half moon-nodes and their connection with the transition in the ninth year. From this point of view, pedagogy becomes an art that has to do with forces and their further development, leading far beyond the narrow limits of mere personality.

The Reversal in the Change of Teeth

If we observe the change of teeth in children, we can see that the principle of reversal as it operates in the ninth year is also at work in the process of teeth formation. Accordingly, we can say that the cosmic picture of reversal that we saw in the movement of the moon, which crosses its own earlier path at the half moon-nodes after nine and one-third years, is reflected not only in the human organism as a whole, but also in the process of tooth formation as well. And in order to help and support this physiological process Rudolf Steiner recommended a truly effective means of assistance in the practice of form drawing. If this is cultivated in exact correspondence with the emergence of the second teeth, then it strengthens the forces building up our body.

The following table shows the sequence in which the second teeth break through; the Arabic numerals refer to the permanent teeth, the Roman numerals to the milk teeth.

6 Years	6	V	IV	III	II	I	I	II	III	IV	V	6
	6	V	IV	III	II	I	I	II	III	IV	V	6
7 Years	6	V	IV	III	II	1	1	II	III	IV	V	6
	6	V	IV	III	II	1	1	II	III	IV	V	6
8 Years	6	V	IV	III	2	1	1	2	III	IV	V	6
	6	V	IV	III	2	1	1	2	III	IV	V	6
9 Years	6	V	4 ⟍ III	2	1	1	2	III	4	V	6
	6	V	IV ⟍ 3	2	1	1	2	3 ⟋ IV	V	6

10 years			6	V	4⟍⟋3	2	1	1	2	3⟍⟋4	V	6		
			6	V	4⟋⟍3	2	1	1	2	3⟋⟍4	V	6		
11 Years			6	5	4	3	2	1	1	2	3	4	5	6
			6	5	4	3	2	1	1	2	3	4	5	6
from 12th Year		7	6	5	4	3	2	1	1	2	3	4	5	6	7
		7	6	5	4	3	2	1	1	2	3	4	5	6	7
from 13th Year	8	7	6	5	4	3	2	1	1	2	3	4	5	6	7	8
	8	7	6	5	4	3	2	1	1	2	3	4	5	6	7	8

A concrete example can show us how the formative forces at work in the change of teeth are brought into play pedagogically in the practice of form drawing.

First grade:
By the age of six, children have produced the no. 6 tooth. In the first grade they acquire the no. 1s. In the movement from side to middle we see the symmetry factor that is also at work in this form:

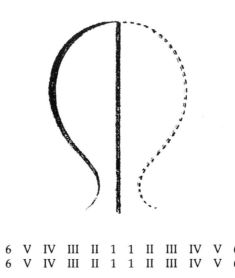

6 V IV III II 1 1 II III IV V 6
6 V IV III II 1 1 II III IV V 6

102

Second grade:
Full harmony emerges now between above and below, right and left, and permanent and milk teeth. A cruciform symmetry is thus established (though at first without any strong connection to the middle):

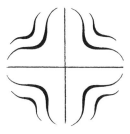

```
6  V  IV  III  2  1  1  2  III  IV  V  6
6  V  IV  III  2  1  1  2  III  IV  V  6
```

Third grade:
The earlier perfect symmetry is broken. Now forms arise that relate to the middle position in a free way and not in strict symmetry. At this age cursive writing can be introduced.

```
6  V  4 III  2  1  1  2  III  4  V  6
6  V  IV  3  2  1  1  2  3  IV  V  6
```

Rudolf Steiner's Indications for Form Drawing in the First Three School Years

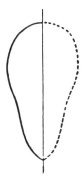

"A beginning can already be made in this connection with the smallest children. For example, you draw this or that figure on the board (dark line), add to it a straight line like this for the children, and draw in a little bit of the symmetry line for them, and try and get the children to see that the drawing is not complete. Have them imagine what is needed to finish it. You try in every way possible to get the children to finish the drawing. In this way, you arouse in the children this inner active urge to complete not only what is unfinished in things, but also to develop within themselves a correct picture of reality in every circumstance. For this sort of thing, the teacher needs to be inventive. It is always good if the teacher possesses flexible, richly inventive thinking; this is what the teacher needs."[1]

"Then you can go on from such things and help the child to see how a reflection comes about. If here there is a water surface and some object or other, you call on the child to imagine how the object is mirrored in the water. In this way, you can gradually lead the child into the harmonies that prevail everywhere in the world."[2]

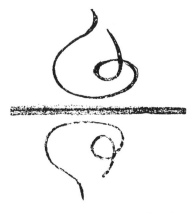

"If the teacher through inventive, flexible thinking has done such exercises for a time, he or she can then move on to others. For example, the teacher can draw such a figure as this, and try to evoke in the child an inner spatial picture of the figure.

"Then the teacher can try to find a transition by drawing the inner figure in such a way that the child comes to see that the inner figure must be made to correspond to the variations in the outer one.

"In the first drawing the line first made just curves out and back; the second line also has outward projections. Now in this next drawing we can make it clear to the children that when they draw the inner figure an inner symmetry must be obtained. They must let the inside line go inward where the outer line projects outward. Thus, whereas in the first drawing the simple line corresponds to the simple line, in the second, the outward curve corresponds to the inward curve. Or we can try the following:

"The teacher can draw this figure (the three inside forms) for the children, and then the corresponding outer forms, so that a harmonious whole is the result. And now he or she tries to find the transition from this figure to one where the outer forms do not come together, but run away from each other, so that they stream out into the indefinite.

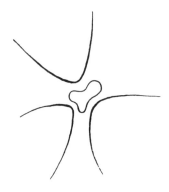

"Now the children get the impression that this point wants to run away from them and that they have to run after it with the lines, but just cannot catch up; the point has simply flown away. Then the children realize that they must arrange the corresponding figure properly, so that, because this ran away, they must turn this form inward in a particular way.

"Here I can only explain the principles involved. In short, we enable the child in this way to visualize asymmetrical symmetries. And thus we prepare the ether body or formative-force-body while the children are awake to continue to vibrate during sleep and, in this vibrating, to perfect what has been achieved during the day. Then in the morning, the children will wake up in an ether body and physical body that are inwardly and organically in movement. That brings a tremendous liveliness into the human being."[3]

Notes

Introduction

[1]Rudolf Steiner, *The Child's Changing Consciousness and Waldorf Education*, (Hudson, New York: Anthroposophic Press, 1988), Lecture V, pp. 103-126.

Conversation with Peter's Parents

[1]The content of the conversation with parents in Chapter 1 and Chapter 2 is a free representation of the essential characteristics of the transition in the ninth year. Any similarities with actual living or dead persons are unintentional and mere coincidence.

[2]Rudolf Steiner, *Human Values in Education* (London: Rudolf Steiner Press, 1971).

[3]See Rudolf Steiner, *The Renewal of Education*, (Forest Row, England: Steiner Schools Fellowship Publications, 1981).

[4]Rudolf Steiner, *Soul Economy and Waldorf Education*, (Spring Valley, New York: Anthroposophic Press, 1986), Lecture X, pp. 162-181.

Dear Parents

[1]Rudolf Steiner, *The Renewal of Education*, (Forest Row, England: Steiner Schools Fellowship Publications, 1981).

[2]Rudolf Steiner, *Kingdom of Childhood*, 2nd ed., (London: Rudolf Steiner Press, 1988) Lecture 2, p. 51:
The reality is this, speaking of course in a general sense: the child of this age approaches his much-loved

teacher, be he man or woman, with some problem or difficulty. In most cases he will not actually speak of what is burdening his soul, but will say something different. All the same one has to know that this really comes from the innermost depths of his soul, and the teacher must then find the right approach, the right answer. An enormous amount depends on this for the whole future life of the child concerned.

3*Christmas Plays from Oberufer*, trsl. A. C. Harwood, (London: Rudolf Steiner Press, 1973), p. 9.

4Rudolf Steiner, *Geisteswissenschaftliche Gesichtspunkte zur Therapie*, No. 313 in the Collected Works, (Dornach, Switzerland: Rudolf Steiner Verlag, 1984), not yet translated.

5Rudolf Steiner, *The Renewal of Education*, (Forest Row, England: Steiner Schools Fellowship Publications, 1981).

6Christian Morgenstern, *Wir fanden einen Pfad: Poems*, Vol. 11 in the Collected Works, (Basel, Switzerland: Zbinden Verlag, 1977), p. 20.

The Ninth Year in Biography

1Walter Johannes Stein, *Weltgeschichte im Lichte des Heiligen Gral: Das neunte Jahrhundert*, (Stuttgart, Germany: Mellinger Verlag, 1966), p. XI.

2Heinrich Schliemann, *Selbstbiographie*, ed. by Sophie Schliemann, (Wiesbaden, Germany: Brockhaus, 1955), p. 20.

3Hans Carossa, *Eine Kindheit*, (Leipzig: Insel Verlag, n.d.), p. 143ff.

4Rudolf Steiner, *Der Tod als Lebenswandlung*, No. 182 in the Collected Works, (Dornach, Switzerland: Rudolf Steiner Verlag, 1976), not yet translated.

5Carossa, *Eine Kindheit*.

6Oskar Kokoschka, *Mein Leben*, (München: Verlag F. Bruckmann, 1972), p. 38.

7Bruno Walter, *Thema und Variationen: Erinnerungen und Gedanken*, (Zürich, 1973), p. 31.

[8]Rudolf Steiner, *The Course of My Life*, (Hudson, New York: Anthroposophic Press, 1986).

[9]Heinz Müller, *Healing Forces in the Word and its Rhythms*, (Forest Row, England: Rudolf Steiner Schools Fellowship Publications, 1983).

[10]Heinz Müller, *Spuren auf dem Weg*, (Stuttgart, Germany: Mellinger Verlag, 1976), p. 11.

[11]Rudolf Steiner, *Mystery Knowledge and Mystery Centres*, 2nd ed., (London: Rudolf Steiner Press, 1973).

[12]Heinz Müller, *Healing Forces in the Word and its Rhythms*, p. 10.

[13]Müller, *Healing Forces*, p. 10.

[14]Müller, *Healing Forces*, p. 11.

[15]Rudolf Steiner, *A Modern Art of Education*, (London: Rudolf Steiner Press, 1972), p. 104.

The Second Seven Years

[1]Rudolf Steiner, *Human Values in Education*, (London: Rudolf Steiner Press, 1971).

[2]H. Matthiolius, M.D., "Basic Elements of the School Physician's Activity", Husemann and Wolff, eds., *The Anthroposophical Approach to Medicine*, vol. I, (Spring Valley, New York: Anthroposophic Press, 1982), pp. 89-120.

Children at Seven and Twelve: A Comparison

[1]Caroline von Heydebrand, *The Curriculum of the First Waldorf School*, repr., (Forest Row, England: Rudolf Steiner Schools Fellowship Publications, 1986), p. 17:
Physics. In this school year the child is ripe for the first physics lesson. Here also the teacher should follow the natural healthy way for the growing child, that is, the way from the artistic to the intellectual. From music the child should be led to acoustics and then the larynx should be described. Colour and painting with which the child has been familiar from the beginning of

school-life should lead on to optics, and to the phenomena of colour and light. The eye should not be discussed. The child is not yet ready to appreciate the application of physical law to the operation of sense organs in a living body. The teaching of Heat, Electricity, and Magnetism can be introduced, starting from phenomena and developing the general laws from them.

²Rudolf Steiner, *The Child's Changing Consciousness and Waldorf Education*, (Hudson, New York: Anthroposophic Press, 1988), p. 65:

The way in which breathing and blood circulation become inwardly harmonized, the way in which the child breathes at school, and the way in which the breathing gradually adapts itself to the blood circulation, all this happens as a rule between the ninth and the tenth year. At first, up to the ninth year, the child's breathing is in the head, until, through an inner struggle within its organism, a kind of harmony between the pulse beat and the breath is established. This is followed by a time when the blood circulation predominates, and this general change takes place in the physical realm and in the realm of the child's soul.

The Child in the Ninth Year Transition

¹See Rudolf Steiner, *Balance in Teaching*, (Spring Valley, New York: Mercury Press, 1982), Lecture II, pp. 15-30; and

Rudolf Steiner, *The Child's Changing Consciousness and Waldorf Education*, (Hudson, New York: Anthroposophic Press, 1988), Lecture V, pp. 103-126.

²Hadumoth Rötges, "Was geschieht im neunten Lebensjahr— geistig-seelisch und körperlich?" in *Erziehungskunst*, No. 3, March 1952.

³Rudolf Steiner, *Geisteswissenschaftliche Gesichtspunkte zur Therapie*, No. 313 in the Collected Works, (Dornach, Switzerland: Rudolf Steiner Verlag, 1984).

⁴Rudolf Steiner, *Practical Advice to Teachers*, repr., (London: Rudolf Steiner Press, 1988), Lecture Seven, pp. 99-114.

⁵Rudolf Steiner, *Soul Economy and Waldorf Education*, (Spring Valley, New York: Anthroposophic Press, 1986), p. 166:
And the way in which a teacher responds to this situation may be a decisive factor for the child's entire life. Whether it will grow up into an unstable character or into a person strongly integrated in life, may well depend on whether the teacher is acting with inner certainty and understanding during this crucial time. See also Rudolf Steiner, *Kingdom of Childhood*, 2nd ed., (London: Rudolf Steiner Press, 1988), p. 52:
And then between the ninth and tenth year this feeling arises instinctively in his subconsciousness: I get everything from my teacher, but where does he get it from? What is behind him? The teacher need not enlarge on this because if you go into definitions and explanations it can only do harm. The important thing is to find a loving word, a word filled with warmth of heart—or rather many words, for these difficulties can go on for weeks and months—so that we can avert this danger and preserve the feeling for authority in the child. For he has now come to a crisis as regards the principle of authority. If you are equal to the situation, and can preserve your authority by the warmth of feeling with which you deal with these particular difficulties, and by meeting the child with inner warmth, sincerity, and truth, then much will be gained. The child will retain his belief in the teacher's authority, and that is a good thing for his further education, but it is also essential that just at this age of life between nine and ten the child's belief in a good person should not waver. Were this to happen then the inner security which should be his guide through life will totter and sway.
This is of very great significance and must constantly be borne in mind. In the handbooks on education we find all kinds of intricate details laid down for the

guidance of teachers, but it is of far greater importance to know what happens at a certain point in the child's life and how we must act with regard to it, so that through our action we may radiate light on to his whole life.

[6]Caroline von Heydebrand, *The Curriculum of the First Waldorf School*, p. 12:

Tone eurythmy. The step should be made from the learning of the simple sharp and flat keys to melodies in these keys. In this connection we need to remember that the child between nine and ten years old stands in the world with a different consciousness from heretofore. Major and minor begin for the first time to have a content in the child's experience. In this way the interval of the major and minor third can be brought to the child. All the same the minor element in music should not be practiced much in Eurythmy for it does not suit the nature of the child of twelve to grasp so deeply the element of music in the earthly human being.

See also: Rudolf Steiner, *The Child's Changing Consciousness and Waldorf Education*, (Hudson, New York: Anthroposophic Press, 1988), pp. 65-66:

And then, between the ninth and tenth year, something really remarkable begins to happen; the child feels more akin to the musical element. The child wants to be gripped by music and rhythms far more than previously. If we observe how the child—up to the point between the ninth and tenth year—responds to music, how the musical element lives in the child as a plastically molding force, and how, as a matter of course, the musical forces are active in the inner sculpting of the physical body . . . If we notice how the child's affinity to music easily expresses itself in an eagerness to perform dance-like movements, then we are bound to recognize that the child's real ability to grasp music begins to evolve between the ninth and tenth year. At that time this becomes clearly noticeable.

Naturally, these things do not fall into strictly separate categories, and if one is able to grasp them completely, one will also cultivate a musical approach before the ninth year, but in an appropriate way. One will tend in the direction suggested just now. Otherwise the child aged nine to ten would get too much of a shock if it were suddenly exposed to the musical element in full force, if it found itself gripped by musical experiences without due preparation.

7Translator's note: This connection is clearer in the German text, where *greifen*, to grasp, appears again in *begreifen*, to understand. *Stellen*, to place, is found in *sich vorstellen*, to imagine, and *nehmen*, to take, in *wahrnehmen*, to perceive.

8Rudolf Steiner, *Kingdom of Childhood*, Lecture 4, pp. 73-88.

9Walter Holtzapfel, M.D., "Aspects of Diagnosis and Therapy for the School Physician," Husemann and Wolff, eds., *The Anthroposophical Approach to Medicine*, vol. I, (Spring Valley, New York: Anthroposophic Press, 1982), pp. 120-131.

10Rudolf Steiner, *Study of Man*, repr., (London: Rudolf Steiner Press, 1981), pp. 23-24:

Truly, my dear friends, it makes a very great difference whether one teacher of the school or another comes through the classroom door to any group of children. There is a big difference; and the difference is not merely that the one teacher is more skilful in his practice than the other. No, the main difference—the one that is really influential in teaching—lies in what the teacher bears within him as his constant trend of thought, and carries with him into the classroom. A teacher who occupies himself with thoughts of the evolving human being will work very differently upon his pupils from a teacher who knows nothing of all these things, and never gives them a thought. Once you begin to know the cosmic significance of the breathing process and of its transformation through education, and the cosmic significance of the rhythm between sleeping and waking—what is it that happens? The moment you have such thoughts something in you is combating your purely personal nature. The moment you have such thoughts the very basis of this spirit of personality is of less effect. In that moment all that enhances a personal spirit is damped down, all that man possesses through the fact that he is a physical man. If you have quenched this personal spirit, then, as you enter the classroom, it will come about through inner forces that a relationship is established between the pupils and yourself.

The Incarnation of the Ego

[1]Rudolf Steiner, *Spiritual Science and Medicine*, repr., (London: Rudolf Steiner Press, 1975).

[2]Rudolf Steiner, *Theosophy: An Introduction to the Supersensible Knowledge of the World and the Destination of Man*, repr., (Hudson, New York: Anthroposophic Press, 1986).

The Half Moon-Nodes

[1]Joachim Schultz, *Movement and Rhythms of the Stars*, (Edinburgh, Scotland: Floris Books, 1986), p. 85ff.

Rudolf Steiner's Indications for Form Drawing

[1]Rudolf Steiner, *A Modern Art of Education*, (London: Rudolf Steiner Press, 1972), Lecture IX, pp. 152-167.

[2]Rudolf Steiner, *Kingdom of Childhood*, Lecture 4, pp. 73-88.

[3]Steiner, *Kingdom of Childhood*, Lecture 4.